INSIGHT'S

BIBLE APPLICATION GUIDE

Job – Song of Solomon

A LIFE LESSON FROM EVERY CHAPTER

From the Bible-Teaching Ministry of
CHARLES R. SWINDOLL

Insight's Bible Application Guide: Job – Song of Solomon
A Life Lesson from Every Chapter
From the Bible-Teaching Ministry of Charles R. Swindoll

Charles R. Swindoll has devoted his life to the accurate, practical teaching and application of God's Word and His grace. A pastor at heart, Chuck has served as senior pastor to congregations in Texas, Massachusetts, and California. Since 1998, he has served as the founder and senior pastor-teacher of Stonebriar Community Church in Frisco, Texas, but Chuck's listening audience extends far beyond a local church body. As a leading program in Christian broadcasting since 1979, *Insight for Living* airs in major Christian radio markets around the world, reaching people groups in languages they can understand. Chuck's extensive writing ministry has also served the body of Christ worldwide and his leadership as president and now chancellor of Dallas Theological Seminary has helped prepare and equip a new generation of men and women for ministry. Chuck and Cynthia, his partner in life and ministry, have four grown children, ten grandchildren, and two great-grandchildren.

Published By: IFL Publishing House, A Division of Insight for Living Ministries,
Post Office Box 1050, Frisco, Texas 75034-0018

Editor in Chief: Cynthia Swindoll, President, Insight for Living Ministries
Executive Vice President: Wayne Stiles, Th.M., D.Min., Dallas Theological Seminary
Writers: John Adair, Th.M., Ph.D., Dallas Theological Seminary
   Malia Rodriguez, Th.M., Dallas Theological Seminary
   Wayne Stiles, Th.M., D.Min., Dallas Theological Seminary
Content Editor: Kathryn Robertson, M.A., English, Hardin-Simmons University
   Amy L. Snedaker, B.A., English, Rhodes College
Copy Editors: Jim Craft, M.A., English, Mississippi College
   Paula McCoy, B.A., English, Texas A&M University-Commerce
   Kathryn Robertson, M.A., English, Hardin-Simmons University
Project Coordinator, Creative Ministries: Megan Meckstroth, B.S., Advertising, University of Florida
Project Coordinator, Publishing: Melissa Cleghorn, B.A., University of North Texas
Proofreader: LeeAnna Smith, B.A., Communications, Moody Bible Institute
Designer: Margaret Gulliford, B.A., Graphic Design, Taylor University
Production Artist: Nancy Gustine, B.F.A., Advertising Art, University of North Texas

Table of Contents

A Letter from Chuck

Our culture suffers no shortage of people with academic degrees, corporate titles, and intellectual know-how. But sadly, wise men and women are still hard to find. Why? It's simple. The pursuit of knowledge, while often good, doesn't always produce wisdom. At least, not automatically.

True wisdom requires us to read God's Word with the goal of practical application, not merely intellectual stimulation. Wisdom applies truth to all of life . . . and that takes a lot of time, including numerous trials as well.

The inspired poets of Psalms, Proverbs, Ecclesiastes, Job, and Song of Solomon—the Wisdom Books—learned how to trust God through the challenges they faced. When hunted by King Saul, David sought the Lord and then praised God when He rescued him. Job endured unimaginable tragedy and ultimately grew to appreciate God's sovereignty. And Solomon finally found the meaning of life in God—only after exhausting every other meaningless avenue. In the midst of their experiences, these writers clung to God's promises and trusted in His faithful character. Years of struggle showed them how to *apply* God's truth to life in its raw reality.

As these writers recorded their insights, they employed a method of Hebrew poetry that seems odd to our twenty-first century ears. Our poetry commonly communicates thoughts through rhythm and rhyme. But Hebrew poetry conveys an author's emotions and experiences through parallel thoughts.

The Wisdom Books employ three main types of parallel lines: *synonymous parallelism*, which repeats one thought in a different way; *antithetic parallelism*, which contrasts two thoughts, often using *but* or *however*; and *synthetic parallelism*, which uses the second line to further develop the idea of the first.

Don't let these unusual terms confuse you! You don't have to master them to read, understand, and apply the truths of biblical poetry. But being aware of how the poets wrote will help you appreciate their craft much more.

Our goal in providing you the *Insight's Bible Application Guide: Job – Song of Solomon* is to give you, in simple terms, a life lesson from every single chapter in the Wisdom Books. I'm confident that the volume you hold in your hand will show you how you can apply these inspired words to your life and gain wisdom in the process.

So, let's begin our journey with Job, David, Solomon, and other biblical poets as we apply these inspired verses of Hebrew poetry.

Charles R. Swindoll

About the Writers

Charles R. Swindoll

Charles R. Swindoll has devoted his life to the accurate, practical teaching and application of God's Word and His grace. A pastor at heart, Chuck has served as senior pastor to congregations in Texas, Massachusetts, and California. Since 1998, he has served as the founder and senior pastor-teacher of Stonebriar Community Church in Frisco, Texas, but Chuck's listening audience extends far beyond a local church body. As a leading program in Christian broadcasting since 1979, *Insight for Living* airs in major Christian radio markets around the world, reaching people groups in languages they can understand. Chuck's extensive writing ministry has also served the body of Christ worldwide and his leadership as president and now chancellor of Dallas Theological Seminary has helped prepare and equip a new generation for ministry. Chuck and Cynthia, his partner in life and ministry, have four grown children, ten grandchildren, and two great-grandchildren. Chuck contributed the chapter on Job.

John Adair

Th.M., Ph.D., Dallas Theological Seminary

John received his master of theology degree from Dallas Theological Seminary, where he also completed his Ph.D. in Historical Theology. He serves as a writer in the Creative Ministries Department of Insight for Living. John, his wife, Laura, and their three children reside in Frisco, Texas. John contributed chapters on Psalms 42–72; 90–150, and Ecclesiastes.

Malia Rodriguez

Th.M., Dallas Theological Seminary

Malia received her master of theology degree in Systematic Theology from Dallas Theological Seminary. She now serves as a writer in the Creative Ministries Department of Insight for Living, where she is able to merge her love of theology with her gift for words. Malia and her husband, Matt, who is also a graduate of Dallas Theological Seminary, live in the Dallas area with their son. Malia contributed chapters on Psalms 1–41; 73–89.

Wayne Stiles

Th.M., D.Min., Dallas Theological Seminary

Wayne received his master of theology in Pastoral Ministries and doctor of ministry in Biblical Geography from Dallas Theological Seminary. In 2005, after serving in the pastorate for fourteen years, Wayne joined the staff at Insight for Living Ministries, where he leads and labors alongside a team of writers, editors, and pastors as the executive vice president and chief content officer. Wayne and his wife, Cathy, live in Aubrey, Texas, and have two daughters in college. Wayne contributed chapters on Proverbs and Song of Solomon.

What Is the Value of the Wisdom Books Today?

Wisdom is one of those slippery concepts—something we all desire but not something that many of us know how to acquire. We can find wisdom in a variety of places, such as our own lifelong experiences and the experiences of others. We can also learn from great art or lasting works of literature. For the Christian, however, one source of wisdom stands above all others: the Bible. Scripture deals with the concept of wisdom most pointedly in the five books we call Wisdom Books—Job through Song of Solomon. What value can we glean from the Wisdom Books?

First, the Wisdom Books tackle one of the most significant questions in all of human history: Why does God allow evil in the world? Job's struggle with the presence of evil in his life remains one of the most poignant portraits of human suffering that pen ever put to paper. After losing virtually everything, Job lamented:

> "I loathe my own life;
> I will give full vent to my complaint;
> I will speak in the bitterness of my soul."
> (Job 10:1)

Job continued to struggle and eventually, God visited him—not with specific answers to Job's questions but with a declaration of His power and presence in the world. The profundity of the book of Job cuts across all human differences. Wherever and whenever we live, Job's plight resonates in the deepest recesses of our souls.

Second, the Wisdom Books point God's people toward worship. In particular, the book of Psalms describes a varied collection of ways in which the biblical writers approached the Lord in worship. Individual laments offer prayers in times of great need or distress, with a confession of trust, a specific petition, and praise to the Lord (Psalm 59). National laments follow the same pattern as individual laments but are focused on God's people as a whole approaching Him due to their trials (Psalm 94). Thanksgiving psalms involve the psalmist giving thanks for God's deliverance and usually include praise to God for His deeds, a recounting of the deliverance, and more praise in light of God's salvation (Psalm 18). Finally, descriptive praise psalms offer God direct praise, usually for His greatness and grace (Psalm 33). While there are other types of psalms used less frequently in the Psalter, the variety of approaches to God gives us all a sense of the ways we, too, might approach the Lord.

Finally, the Wisdom Books tackle intensely practical questions. Proverbs includes advice on any number of everyday topics such as hard work (Proverbs 10:4), temper (14:17), and the proper use of the tongue (16:24). This practical book details principles for us to live by rather than promises for God to keep. Ecclesiastes offers a dark meditation on life that concludes with good advice by which all of us can order our lives — fear God and obey His commands (Ecclesiastes 12:13). And Song of Solomon presents a portrait of marital love, delving into one of the most significant relationships in the entire human experience.

Without wisdom in our lives, we have only one alternative: foolishness (Proverbs 10:23; 12:15; 14:3). As followers of Jesus, we want to avoid such an undesirable trait. Appreciating the beauty of God's Wisdom Books and heeding their advice will help us to achieve God's desires in our lives, ultimately allowing us to find joy, satisfaction, and wisdom in Him.

INSIGHT'S
BIBLE APPLICATION GUIDE
Job – Song of Solomon
A LIFE LESSON FROM EVERY CHAPTER

Job

Job 1

Then the LORD said to Satan, "Behold, all that he has is in your power, only do not put forth your hand on him." So Satan departed from the presence of the LORD.   —*Job 1:12*

Job was a man of unparalleled and genuine piety. He was also a man of well-deserved prosperity. He was a godly gentleman, a wise businessman, a fine husband, and a faithful father. In a quick and brutal sweep of back-to-back calamities, Job was reduced to a twisted mass of brokenness and grief. Why did God allow Job to go through so much pain? Christians must learn that life includes trials that we do not deserve but must endure. In the mystery of God's unfathomable will, we can never explain or fully understand what He's doing. If we try to grasp each thread of His profound plan, we will become confused, resentful, and bitter. At that point, Satan will have defeated us. We must accept and endure the trials that God permits, knowing that nothing touches our lives that hasn't first been allowed by God. Do we trust Him enough to accept this truth?

Job 2

But he said to her, "You speak as one of the foolish women speaks. Shall we indeed accept good from God and not accept adversity?" In all this Job did not sin with his lips.   —*Job 2:10*

The second chapter of Job starts as ominously as the first. Satan likes to hit humanity with double punches. For Job, the first punch came as a complete surprise; the second one hit him with stunning shock. As before, Satan fully intended to ruin Job *so that Job would curse God.* Having also lost her children and wealth, even Job's wife told him to curse God. Satan's victory or defeat hung on Job's response. But Job said, in effect,

"No, no, no, sweetheart. We serve God, who has the right to do whatever He pleases and is never obligated to explain it or ask our permission." Christians must remember that God has a plan that is beyond our comprehension. Our role is to maintain our integrity and refuse to curse God.

Job 3

"Let the day perish on which I was to be born,
And the night which said, 'A boy is conceived.'"   —Job 3:3

The man had reached the end of his rope. Job's outburst in chapter 3 did not flow primarily out of his physical suffering. It was emotional—he had lost touch with God. For many years, Job had experienced intimacy with God . . . until that awful day when everything broke loose and Job lost nearly everything. Then, the real darkness came. The heavens turned to brass, impenetrable and unyielding. Against God's silence, Job opened the floodgates, pouring out his internal turmoil on God. Job even cursed the day he was born! But in spite of Job's fit, God didn't blast Job into oblivion. God didn't even say, "Shame on you, Job." God can handle our tough questions and emotional outbursts. When we face pain too deep for words, we can share it with God. We'll never get over grief until we express it fully to Him. So don't hold back—the Lord can handle it.

Job 4

"Remember now, who ever perished being innocent?
Or where were the upright destroyed?"   —Job 4:7

Not all advice is good advice. Sometimes counsel is given in all sincerity, but it is still faulty. While in his deep depression,

Job had some visitors. Job's three friends spent seven days with him in silence, watching, listening, and forming their opinions about Job's situation. When they opened their mouths, things only got worse. They mixed blame and shame, condemnation and judgment. They heaped on Job loads of legalism, and to drive their point home, they resorted to sarcasm and argument. They lost sight of their purpose — to *sympathize* and *comfort* (Job 2:11). Sometimes the words of others only complicate our lives and make our troubles worse. Few traps are more disastrous than the trap of believing everything we hear. So when we're in desperate need of advice, let's pick our counselors carefully and make sure we don't give equal weight to everyone's advice. We must filter all advice through God's Word, prayer, and common sense.

Job 5

"Behold, how happy is the man whom God reproves,
So do not despise the discipline of the Almighty."   —*Job 5:17*

Job's three friends Eliphaz, Bildad, and Zophar took turns dialoguing with Job. After the first cycle, Eliphaz came back on the scene to start the second cycle. After accusing and shaming Job, Eliphaz had the audacity to say, "Do not despise the discipline of the Almighty" (Job 5:17). Don't miss the implication: "You're suffering because you're guilty, Job! You're getting just what you deserve. Once you repent of your sins, you'll be just fine." Somewhere in that bad sermon, accusation overran compassion. Because suffering is part of our world, all believers will have the opportunity to comfort others. But if we don't have a clear mind, please, let's just love our hurting friends and keep silent. Let's vow not to follow the relentless, heartless preaching of Job's "friends." Let's care for the hurting by listening, serving, and praying.

Job 6

"But it is still my consolation,
And I rejoice in unsparing pain,
That I have not denied the words of the Holy One."   *—Job 6:10*

Finally, Eliphaz finished his long-winded, cruel speech. Job responded, in effect, "I want you to understand, Eliphaz, that in all of this—hating the day I was born and swinging my fist at the fact that I didn't die beyond birth and sinking in unbearable misery—I've never once sinned against God with my lips." That's quite a statement. And it was a fact. Though Job suffered, he didn't deny his faith in God. Was he confused? Yes. Angry? Of course. But Eliphaz hadn't given Job a chance. He had only made assumptions and accusations. It's vital that we give our fellow Christians room to feel confused and to express anger in hard times. Being a good counselor requires impeccable timing, great wisdom, and deep understanding. We must put ourselves in our brothers' and sisters' shoes and love them as we would want to be loved.

Job 7

"I waste away; I will not live forever.
Leave me alone, for my days are but a breath."   *—Job 7:16*

An endeavor that began for all the right reasons got lost in the shuffle of time and tension. It wasn't long before the words of Job's friends became lectures laced with shame and sarcasm. Job needed them near as compassionate friends, but instead they bristled with caustic comments and accusations. The words of Job's friends had added more pain to his already unbearable agony. Finally, Job begged them to leave him alone. Eliphaz, Bildad, and Zophar kept offering their shallow answers and simplistic solutions as Job struggled to survive. When suffering friends and family need our love and compassion, philosophical words will only increase their misery. The longer we try to explain another person's suffering, the further we will drift from helping that person at a time when he or she *desperately* needs us! Unlike Job's friends, who caused him to lose hope, we can bring refreshment and nonjudgmental care to the suffering.

Job 8

"If your sons sinned against Him,
Then He delivered them into the power of their transgression."

—Job 8:4

We can't forget that as Job eloquently defended himself against his friend's assault, he was a grieving father who had lost *all* of his children. So when we read Job 8:4, our hearts break with Job's. Not only was he grief-stricken over the loss of his children, he had to listen to this man who had the audacity to say that their deaths were due to God's punishing them for their transgressions. To make matters worse, Bildad claimed to speak for God. It's amazing that Job didn't punch Bildad right in the face! But Job, being a man of heroic endurance, restrained himself. Job's silence was remarkable. When we get hit unfairly and repeatedly, how do we respond? Do we reciprocate cruelty, or do we entrust ourselves to the Lord, allowing Him to defend us? Sometimes our silence reveals more about our faith than do our words.

Job 9

"For He is not a man as I am that I may answer Him,
That we may go to court together.
There is no umpire between us,
Who may lay his hand upon us both."   *—Job 9:32–33*

Even though he knew he was innocent, Job patiently endured Bildad's cruel accusations and theological sermonizing. Job longed for an arbitrator who could argue his case before God. Job didn't qualify to stand before the Lord on his own because Job wasn't Deity, and God is not a man that He could stand before Job — so Job was stuck. Would that Job had lived many centuries later — after the life, death, and resurrection of Christ! Paul wrote of the Mediator between us and God — "the man Christ Jesus" (1 Timothy 2:5). We're surrounded by people searching for hope, trying to make it through the maze of misery. Many of them long for someone who can represent their cause and plead their case, someone who can bridge the gap between them and God. Let's point them to the Mediator — Jesus. Anyone who comes to Him for comfort will find it. He has far more mercy than we have misery.

Job 10

"I loathe my own life;
I will give full vent to my complaint;
I will speak in the bitterness of my soul."   *—Job 10:1*

Dark clouds don't dissipate quickly. In chapter 10, Job still struggled. Eliphaz had left him cold, Bildad offered neither comfort nor insight, and Job had no mediator to represent his case to God. Confused and sad, the broken man returned to questions he had asked earlier: *Why didn't God just take me from the womb and carry me to the tomb?* Job was back where he started—in the doldrums. Those gloomy clouds still hung low, blocking all light. Darkness plagued his life. The chapter ends sadly. Job shared his struggle, Bildad frowned and walked away, and God remained silent. When depression closes in and our spirits are crushed, we long to hear God's voice. But when God doesn't alleviate our suffering quickly, will we keep on trusting Him? The Lord doesn't owe us answers. And He doesn't promise happiness in life. But He does assure us of hope beyond our pain. We must choose to believe His Word and walk by faith.

Job 11

"If iniquity is in your hand, put it far away,
And do not let wickedness dwell in your tents;
Then, indeed, you could lift up your face without moral defect,
And you would be steadfast and not fear."   —*Job 11:14–15*

Job's third friend, Zophar, was a classic legalist, and he made a classic legalist error in response to tragedy. While he correctly acknowledged the infinitude and greatness of God and correctly urged Job to understand such truths, Zophar then exhorted Job to shape up. Zophar arrogantly assumed Job knew something he wasn't willing to admit. Job must have been keeping his sins a secret, and Zophar was bound and determined to expose them. Like Zophar, we can be terribly judgmental, presuming to know why others are going through hard times. Furthermore, we can paint with too broad a brush, assuming that sin must be at the root of their depression. But that's not always the case. We need to stay with the facts and not allow ourselves to yield to suspicions or jump to false conclusions. It is unfair to see someone as guilty because God's judgment *seems* to have fallen on them.

Job 12

"With Him are wisdom and might;
To Him belong counsel and understanding."   —Job 12:13

Finally, Job had endured enough! Having learned a little sarcasm from his friends, Job responded to them, in effect: "You people really know everything, don't you? And when you die, wisdom will die with you!" (Job 12:2 NLT). Job had talked with the Living God and understood who He really was, and yet Job's friends thought he was a joke. So Job demonstrated his knowledge. He declared something along the lines of, "It is all about our God! It is the inscrutable, almighty God who is in charge of all things. The God I serve takes delight in undoing human activities, in dismantling human enterprises and, in the process, executing His miraculous undertakings. He alone is in full control" (see Job 12:13–25). Do we trust that, even in the midst of our suffering, God is still on His throne, completely sovereign? When doubt begins to creep in, let's declare—*out loud*—our faith in God.

Job 13

"Will You cause a driven leaf to tremble?
Or will You pursue the dry chaff?"   —Job 13:25

Job came to the absolute end of himself. Faced with the reality of his condition, he recognized his frailty and his mortality. Job used several word pictures to describe humanity. All humans are frail like leaves. And our days will draw to an end like rotting food. This was honest, unguarded vulnerability. Job didn't envision himself ever getting better. So he settled in, and instead of skimming the surface, dived deep into the waters of intimacy with God. When pain presses us down, it's natural to push back. But God is in control and has a purpose for our suffering. Let's not run from hardship or seek a friend who'll help us get out from under it quickly. Let's stay there. The Lord God will get us through it. And as a result, we'll stop skating on the surface and get to know our suffering Savior on the deepest level.

Job 14

"If a man dies, will he live again?
All the days of my struggle I will wait
Until my change comes."   —*Job 14:14*

Finally, the clouds started to disperse. After searching the earth for hope and coming up empty, Job turned his eyes to eternity. Job lived during the patriarchal era, the time of Abraham, Isaac, and Jacob, when the progress of revelation had hardly begun. Even though Job knew very little about the doctrine of resurrection, something in him longed for life after death. What Job wrote was not meant to reveal all there is to know about resurrection. We have a whole Bible full of further truth. As Christians, we now know that when we die, we will live on. Just as Jesus Christ looked past the pain he would have to face on the cross to the joy awaiting Him on the other side of resurrection, we can face suffering with confidence (see Hebrews 12:2).

With the fullness of revelation at our fingertips in the Bible, let's look to our hope-filled future when pain will no longer darken our world.

Job 15

"Indeed, you do away with reverence
And hinder meditation before God.
For your guilt teaches your mouth,
And you choose the language of the crafty.
Your own mouth condemns you, and not I;
And your own lips testify against you."   —*Job 15:4–6*

In chapter 15, Eliphaz took off the gloves and started swinging bare-fisted with words that cut to the quick. There was not a hint of grace coming from His mouth. This style of communication is not unusual with those who lack understanding. Eliphaz's words held insult, condemnation, and sarcasm. When we're down, graceless people kick us. When we're drowning, they pull us under. When we're confused, they complicate our lives. So what can we possibly learn from the cruel, condemning words of Eliphaz? Through Job's heroic endurance, may the Lord teach us the value of *grace*. Grace is *always* appropriate. *All* of us need it. The person sitting next to us at church on Sunday, the woman pushing that cart in the grocery store, the man putting gas in his car at the next pump. We have no idea what those people may be going through. If we did, we would *want* to demonstrate compassion and grace.

Job 16

"Is there no limit to windy words?
Or what plagues you that you answer?
I too could speak like you,
If I were in your place.
I could compose words against you
And shake my head at you."   —Job 16:3–4

Job was downright disgusted with Eliphaz . . . and rightly so. Job didn't sit there and take another punch in the face by these insulting, proud men. His self-respect stepped in. Bluntly, he responded: "Sorry comforters are you all" (Job 16:2). How's that for an opening line? Sometimes graceless, insulting people just don't get a clue unless we respond to them with equal strength. There are occasions when, like Job, we have to plant a firm verbal blow. In those times, to be sure we're fully understood, we must fight fire with fire. That's why Job informed his friends that they were "sorry comforters." He didn't smile and act pious—he responded truthfully. His integrity was revealed in his honesty. Speaking the truth cuts through the fuzzy, feel-good verbiage that often characterizes religious clichés and keeps us from realizing our need to change. That's why believers must learn to speak the truth in love.

Job 17

"My spirit is broken, my days are extinguished,
The grave is ready for me.
Surely mockers are with me,
And my eye gazes on their provocation."   —Job 17:1–2

Once again, Job poured out his heart to God. Job despaired of life. He longed for death. He was depressed, and how could anyone be surprised? No counselor can be in that line of work very long before meeting with someone who is distressed over the way God has treated him or her. That person's words are strong, full of anguish, because he or she doesn't understand how a loving, gracious God could stay silent and allow such devastating events to happen to one of His own. Remember, Job didn't know the arrangement between Satan and God. And not once did God give Job a word of explanation. When the bottom drops out, how do we respond? In unguarded moments, when our spirits are broken, when God seems absent, do we give up on God? Job's legacy teaches us to persevere in our faith, despite the odds.

Job 18

"Indeed, the light of the wicked goes out,
And the flame of his fire gives no light.
The light in his tent is darkened,
And his lamp goes out above him." —Job 18:5–6

Here's the way Bildad thought: *God is just and fair. If you repent, God will bless you and relieve your affliction. If you don't repent, He'll keep judging you and your pain will continue.* But here's the snag: Job didn't need to repent, because he hadn't done anything wrong. Bildad's theology didn't leave room for mystery. He forgot that, because God is sovereign and all-powerful, He can keep anyone healthy if He wants to. But, for reasons beyond our comprehension, God permits pain. Whether or not we understand this isn't the point. The point is, God is in charge, and that means we're not! The apostle Paul prayed three times that the thorn in his flesh would be removed. And the Lord answered, "No." (see 2 Corinthians 12:7–10). Paul not only stopped praying for relief, he accepted God's firm no as final. May we, like Paul and Job, willingly accept God's mysterious will, trusting His character rather than our feelings.

Job 19

"How long will you torment me
And crush me with words?
These ten times you have insulted me;
You are not ashamed to wrong me."   —*Job 19:2–3*

Job used four passionate verbs to explain what Bildad's words had done: *torment, crush, insult,* and *wrong.* What brutal blows Job took from Bildad's sharp tongue! Unfortunately, people like Bildad still roam around wrecking others with their potent, verbal weapons. The most treacherous enemy in the church is the human tongue. The Bible presents the tongue as a sword that thrusts its way into others' lives, causing deep, lingering hurt (James 3:1–12). Some of us have been verbally assaulted by foes, family members, or even spouses. Instead of using their tongues to affirm and encourage us, they used their tongues to cut us down. Tragically, some of us have been the ones with abusive tongues in our relationships, slicing others with sarcastic, snide remarks. Whether we have received or caused this kind of pain, let's go to the Lord to find comfort, forgiveness, and the courage to make it right.

Job 20

"That the triumphing of the wicked is short,
And the joy of the godless momentary?
Though his loftiness reaches the heavens,
And his head touches the clouds,
He perishes forever like his refuse;
Those who have seen him will say, 'Where is he?'"   —*Job 20:5–7*

Zophar believed it was his responsibility to accuse Job of being wicked and tell him that judgment would come soon. Zophar had three messages for Job: the wicked do not live long, the pleasures of the wicked are temporal, and God's judgment falls hard on the wicked. There was one main problem with those messages: they didn't apply to Job! False accusations were leveled against many other innocent people in Scripture: Joseph, Moses, David, Nehemiah, Peter, Paul, and of course Jesus, who was "a man of sorrows and acquainted with grief" (Isaiah 53:3). Believers today who have been falsely accused should read and re-read the words of Jesus in Matthew 5:11–12, where He called "blessed" those who are the brunt of lies because of their association with Him. Don't miss the promise: the heavenly reward for such Christians will be great. Today, their misery may be enormous, but eternal comfort awaits.

Job 21

"One dies in his full strength,
Being wholly at ease and satisfied;
His sides are filled out with fat,
And the marrow of his bones is moist."   —*Job 21:23–24*

Job's response to Zophar was impressive. Zophar's words warning Job that his wickedness would result in swift death, were insulting, exaggerated, and inappropriate. And Job didn't take it on the chin. The lies needed to be confronted and the accusations denied. Job asked Zophar to prove that the godless always suffer calamity. Just because they don't have the Lord God in their lives doesn't mean that all in that camp go to early graves. Christians need to erase from our minds the stereotyped images of lost people. They're not always depressed, empty, and miserable. Sometimes they are happy, wealthy, and enjoying loving relationships. Never forget that our good news is about the life *beyond.* Our theology needs to be clearly understood and articulated apart from economic lifestyles, personal preferences, or narrow-minded prejudices that suggest the wealthy can never be godly or the poor can never be wicked. Let's conform our views to Scripture.

Job 22

"Is it because of your reverence that He reproves you,
That He enters into judgment against you?
Is not your wickedness great,
And your iniquities without end?"   —*Job 22:4 – 5*

Job had suffered greatly. On top of all of this, came the frowning presence of his friends, who were determined to wrench a confession of guilt from him. Throughout Job 3 – 37 the merciless, monotonous assault continued. After two complete speeches, Eliphaz came back for round three. He didn't cut Job any slack. In fact, Eliphaz's criticism intensified. He called Job a hypocrite, guilty of hiding his sins. It was hard enough for Job to be called a sinner, but to be charged with hypocrisy was a low blow. But Job, who was the antithesis of a hypocrite, kept quiet and didn't return a wicked response. Our God despises hypocrisy. But Christians shouldn't accuse others of hypocrisy unless they have all their facts straight! And we must remember—if *we* are hiding sin, *we* are the hypocrites. Let's ask God to search our hearts and help us to do what is right with humility.

Job 23

"Would He contend with me by the greatness of His power?
No, surely He would pay attention to me.
There the upright would reason with Him;
And I would be delivered forever from my Judge."   —*Job 23:6–7*

As chapter 23 opens, we observe Job's calm, vulnerable prayer. He said, in effect, "I am unable to locate the presence of God, but I trust you, Lord!" Hidden within Job's passionate words is one of the many great characteristics of our God. Even after all Job had been through, he was confident God would not reject or ignore him (Job 23:6–7). When we come to God as we are, we never hear Him shout, "Shame on you!" God hears our pleading, our feelings of need, and He responds, "I love you. I commend you for facing the truth." Christians can learn a valuable lesson from the way God responds to us. When people come to us, open and vulnerable with their confessions, there is one appropriate three-word response: *I forgive you.* People don't need to be put on the spot or shamed because they failed. They need the assurance of forgiveness.

Job 24

"From the city men groan,
And the souls of the wounded cry out;
Yet God does not pay attention to folly."   —*Job 24:12*

In his divinely inspired journal, Job declared his trust in the Lord, even though Job couldn't understand why God had allowed such evil in his life. In chapter 24, Job lists wrongs, failures, and injustices that God had allowed. Robberies, sexual sins, and hidden wrongs were done in the dark, and where was

God? Job may have thought, "I don't know why, but I think God allows these things for purposes beyond my understanding. And I trust Him." Christians must learn the lesson that Job teaches: though God can be elusive and mysterious, strange and silent, invisible and seemingly passive, He is trustworthy. In light of that, let's practice these three principles. First, because only God knows, resist the temptation to explain everything. Second, because God leads, focus on the future benefits, not the present pain. And third, because God is in control, embrace the sovereignty of the Almighty.

Job 25

"Dominion and awe belong to Him
Who establishes peace in His heights."   *—Job 25:2*

Once again, Bildad attempted to explain the unexplainable. Like many of us who were reared in the church, he believed that God has a "wonderful plan" for our lives and always punishes evil right away. Sounds good . . . yet, in the account of Job's life, God captures our attention, makes us wonder, and confuses us. God permitted Satan to afflict a godly servant, while God kept His distance, remained silent, and refused to answer Job's pleas for an explanation. That seems downright cruel. Why? Because the picture many of us were given in Sunday school is incomplete. In Romans 11:33, Paul called God's ways "unsearchable" and "unfathomable." Now, that doesn't mean God isn't good, loving, and merciful. It means that God is also incomprehensible. His ways are beyond us. The longer we study Scripture, the more we realize there is a lot about God we humans simply can't understand.

Job 26

"Behold, these are the fringes of His ways;
And how faint a word we hear of Him!
But His mighty thunder, who can understand?"   —*Job 26:14*

In an intriguing change of roles, Job became Bildad's teacher. It's almost as if Job decided, "You don't have any answers, so let me tell *you* about the infinite, incomprehensible God, who hasn't revealed all the whys and wherefores of His activities." Job communicated a fascinating, cosmological explanation, starting with the departed spirits under the waters all the way up to the pillars of heaven (Job 26:5, 11). Job's lesson revealed that he had a relationship with God that Bildad had never heard of. And because of that relationship, Job could rely on God for whatever he needed. Believers today can learn from Job that we can find great comfort when we rely on God in simple faith. We trust. We stay strong. We pray so we can make it through the challenges life throws at us. As Christians, we must remember that God is the Potter; we are the clay. We are the servants; He is the Master.

Job 27

"For as long as life is in me,
And the breath of God is in my nostrils,
My lips certainly will not speak unjustly,
Nor will my tongue mutter deceit."   —*Job 27:3–4*

The single most important one to Job was his God. And one priority emerged in Job's life that helped him value his relationship with the Lord above all else. Job made thinking God's thoughts his highest goal, especially when his life crumbled. Consider Job's situation: bankrupt, childless, friendless, and diseased. Covered with boils, he lived with a high fever and constant pain. On top of that, he was misunderstood, blamed for secret sins, and rejected by those who once respected him. How in the world did he go on? Job's view of God—not what others thought of him—kept him going. Like Job, Christians must think biblically and theologically. One way to do this is to practice the spiritual discipline of Scripture memorization. We cannot think God's thoughts more acutely than when we quote His very words back to Him during life's difficult situations.

Job 28

"And to man He said, 'Behold, the fear of the Lord, that is wisdom; And to depart from evil is understanding.'" —Job 28:28

Suffering enabled Job to grasp deep truths about God. Suffering helped Job clarify his priorities and focus on the right objectives. The deeper Job's pain, the clearer his vision became. Then he was able to determine what really matters. During the whole process, he learned to replace knowledge with wisdom. But Job knew that seeking wisdom through human effort was a waste of time. True wisdom is looking from God's point of view and seeing life as God sees it. That's why it's so valuable to think God's thoughts, which requires us to know His Word. When we suffer, it's tempting to quit trusting God. But like Job, let's keep forming our priorities according to what really matters. Let's spend less time in the news and more time in Scripture. When we do, God will dictate our agendas and help us interpret suffering and injustice in the light of His wisdom.

Job 29

"Oh that I were as in months gone by,
As in the days when God watched over me;
When His lamp shone over my head,
And by His light I walked through darkness;
As I was in the prime of my days,
When the friendship of God was over my tent."   *—Job 29:2–4*

Finally Job took a break from listening to his so-called friends, and instead reflected on his life. He looked back with pleasant nostalgia as he recounted the blessings of God. What glorious days they were! Job remembered when he had his ten children with him, when they could all visit with him, enjoy meals together, and relax on special days of celebration with everyone around the table. Job's world was so good. Life was so delightful. Joy was everywhere to be found. God's grace abounded. When tragedy hits, let's remember that reflecting on past blessings gives us reason to rejoice in God's goodness. Let's pause long enough to think back. Let's resist all temptation to name the things that did not work out well. Like Job, let's go back to the blessings and camp there. That kind of reflection will lift our spirits and keep us from becoming negative.

Job 30

"I cry out to You for help, but You do not answer me;
I stand up, and You turn Your attention against me.
You have become cruel to me;
With the might of Your hand You persecute me.
You lift me up to the wind and cause me to ride;
And You dissolve me in a storm."   *—Job 30:20–22*

Job had previously enjoyed wealth, honor, meaningful relationships, and intimacy with God. But that was then. Perhaps

Job blinked through tears as he pulled back the sleeve of his robe exposing swollen, itching boils. His lips were cracked and bleeding. The great place of honor Job held in the community had eroded, and his wealth was only a memory. Job no longer enjoyed God's blessings. After recalling his glory days, Job had to face his present reality. He humbly acknowledged what his life had become. When Christians rehearse our present trials, it forces us to swallow our pride. Pride prompts us to look down on others because we have an elevated opinion of our own importance. As followers of Christ, who was known for His perfect humility, we must reflect on the trials we're going through and allow them to appropriately cut us down to size.

Job 31

"If I have walked with falsehood,
And my foot has hastened after deceit,
Let Him weigh me with accurate scales,
And let God know my integrity."   —Job 31:5–6

Job had faced his circumstances with humility. Now, he continued to write in his divinely inspired journal, recording his consistent record of uprightness. Job listed one example after another in which he said, in effect, "I'm not guilty. I've reflected on my past glory. I've rehearsed my present misery, but I want to tell you, I have every reason to reaffirm my present integrity. My integrity is intact." In Job's life, there was no secret lust, no lying, no adultery, no oppression, no lack of compassion, no materialism. As believers today, reaffirming our commitment to integrity will strengthen us with confidence and courage. Like Job, we must hold fast to our integrity in the midst of pain. We must refuse the temptation to view suffering as an excuse to indulge in sins that might bring us temporary relief. Often, suffering reveals how holy we really are.

Job 32

"Behold, I waited for your words,
I listened to your reasonings,
While you pondered what to say.
I even paid close attention to you;
Indeed, there was no one who refuted Job,
Not one of you who answered his words."   —*Job 32:11–12*

Finally, Job got some relief from his three other friends. Elihu, who had been silent, could hold his tongue no longer. The major theme of Elihu's long-winded speech can be stated in three words: *God is sovereign.* God is not only good all the time; He is *in control* all the time. *Even when we're sick?* Yes. *Even when we can't understand why?* Yes. Do we believe that? God is never shocked or surprised by calamity or disease. Our lives are never out of His control. And furthermore, God isn't obligated to explain Himself. The truth is, even if He did, most of us still wouldn't get it, because His ways are deep and His plan is profound. Can we learn to trust our heavenly Father even when He doesn't answer yes to every prayer . . . and even when He doesn't explain why?

Job 33

"Why do you complain against Him
That He does not give an account of all His doings?
Indeed God speaks once,
Or twice, yet no one notices it."   —*Job 33:13–14*

Elihu told Job, in essence: "God has not been silent, but His message is not as you had expected. God may be invisible and seem uninvolved, but He is at work. Are you hearing what He has to say?" Elihu explained a couple of ways that God speaks. God speaks when we're sick. When we're laid aside with anguishing pain, the Lord gets through to us. God communicates in suffering. And, Elihu said, God speaks in supernatural ways. In Job's era, before the Bible was complete, God frequently revealed His message through dreams and visions. Regarding this point, a word of caution is needed. God rarely speaks in dreams and visions these days. There is hardly a need for such revelations, now that Scripture is complete. So when we're tempted to look for signs, visions, and supernatural dreams to find answers to our deep longings, let's turn instead to God's Word.

Job 34

"'Job ought to be tried to the limit,
Because he answers like wicked men.
For he adds rebellion to his sin;
He claps his hands among us,
And multiplies his words against God.'"   —*Job 34:36–37*

Furious with the interchanges he had witnessed between Job and his other friends, Elihu repeated four times that he was burning with anger (Job 32:1–5). He was mad at Job for holding on to his integrity, and he was mad at Job's three friends because they had no answer for Job. Elihu's anger led him to say some cruel things in chapter 34, including calling Job a wicked rebel in need of judgment! We can all remember times when we blurted something out in a fit of anger. During those outbursts, we said many things we wish we hadn't. Somewhere along the way, we also may have said a few things that needed to be said, but their effectiveness was lost because we said them in the wrong way. Let's exercise wisdom as we confront others, and let's pray that the Spirit would help us stay under control.

Job 35

"And now, because He has not visited in His anger,
Nor has He acknowledged transgression well,
So Job opens his mouth emptily;
He multiplies words without knowledge." —Job 35:15–16

Elihu built a case that the reason for God's silence toward Job was that Job had impure motives. And Elihu concluded with harsh words directed, of course, to Job—who was still in pain! Among many communication errors, Elihu made one glaring mistake. He left out humility. We don't read his words very long before we hear pride oozing between the lines. Elihu stated his opinion with too much dogmatism, he saw himself as the final authority, and he left little room for Job's response. Elihu didn't merely speak; he preached at Job! Believers must learn from Elihu that when we're talking one-on-one or to a small group, we're to leave the preaching to someone else. When talking with kids, spouses, or coworkers, we shouldn't preach. Preaching isn't appropriate in intimate settings. What *is* appropriate? Humility, a listening ear, and compassionate words.

Job 36

"Behold, God is exalted in His power;
Who is a teacher like Him?
Who has appointed Him His way,
And who has said, 'You have done wrong?'" —Job 36:22–23

A surprising change occurred in the closing part of Elihu's speech. He got back on target and delivered some reliable truth.

In fact, here he made more sense and spoke with greater accuracy than did any of the others who had spoken earlier. Elihu pointed out that God protectively watches over the righteous; lets the righteous know if they have committed a transgression; and restores them if they respond to His rod of discipline. And if they persist in wrongdoing, they will surely suffer the consequences. Outstanding theology! Too bad Elihu wasted time and effort meandering in so many needless directions before arriving at his destination. When interacting with Christian brothers and sisters who are in pain, let's encourage them with good theology. But as we do, let's make sure that we speak with a kindness that inspires others to know and trust the living God.

Job 37

"The Almighty — we cannot find Him;
He is exalted in power
And He will not do violence to justice and abundant righteousness.
Therefore men fear Him;
He does not regard any who are wise of heart."   —Job 37:23 – 24

Elihu's final words provide a magnificent segue into the moment when God finally broke the silence and revealed Himself to Job in chapter 38. Elihu reminded Job that God is prominent and preeminent. He is majestic in His power, magnificent in His person, and marvelous in His purposes. How refreshing to step back into the shadows of our own insignificance and give full attention to the greatness of our God! *It's all about Him!* We take a step in our maturity when we finally realize life is not about us. It's all about God's glory. Without God, there is no righteousness, no holiness, no promise of forgiveness, no source of absolute truth, no reason to endure, and no hope beyond the grave. May we never forget that nothing compares to our God! Out of devotion, we are to take time to worship Him, bow down before Him, and exalt His name in words, in silence, and in song.

Job 38

"Who is this that darkens counsel
By words without knowledge?
Now gird up your loins like a man,
And I will ask you, and you instruct Me!" —Job 38:2–3

God doesn't always tiptoe into our world, making His presence known in a gentle manner. When God broke the silence with Job, He bolted forth "out of the whirlwind" (Job 38:1). Interestingly, God did not give Job any answers to his questions, nor did God apologize for His silence. He didn't offer a hint of information about the interchange between Himself and Satan. Furthermore, God didn't acknowledge that Job had been through deep struggles. When God finally spoke, He started with reproof. Like Job, Christians tend to become independent and arrogant when we've had to defend ourselves against other people's criticism. We get a little defensive and overconfident. And God has to get our hearts right before He will communicate with us. Even though the Lord sometimes takes drastic measures to stop us in our tracks and remind us that He is in charge. But when we yield to God, He will prepare our hearts to hear Him.

Job 39

"Is it by your understanding that the hawk soars,
Stretching his wings toward the south?
Is it at your command that the eagle mounts up
And makes his nest on high?" —*Job 39:26 – 27*

God asked Job quite a set of questions! We might link it to being in a classroom where the subject is way over our heads and the professor is *way* ahead of us. We have zero answers, so we duck behind the person in front of us, hoping we won't be seen. But God did see Job, and the questions continued. God introduced Himself as the creator and sustainer of the animal kingdom. God set free the wild donkey, bound up the wild ox, empowered the horses, and gave the hawk the ability to soar. But what in the world did a trip to the local zoo have to do with comforting Job, the grieving man with boils all over his skin? God had to remind Job that because He cares intimately for the animals He created, He intimately cared for Job too. Does God not care for us much more than the animals He created (Matthew 6:26)?

Job 40

"Behold, I am insignificant; what can I reply to You?
I lay my hand on my mouth.
Once I have spoken, and I will not answer;
Even twice, and I will add nothing more." —*Job 40:4 – 5*

If we analyze Job's words in chapter 40 verses 4 and 5, we see that he had three responses to the Lord's interrogation. The first—putting his hand over his mouth—was a response of humility. The second was a response of relief. And the third was a response of surrender. That's all God wanted Job to do. And what an important change for Job! Without realizing it, he had become an independent, determined, self-assured apologist for himself. Job had started to appear as if he understood the providence of God. So, what can we learn from Job's transformation? First, because God's ways are higher than ours, regardless of what He allows, we should bow before Him in submission. From that attitude comes true humility. Second, because God is in full control, regardless of where He directs our steps, we should follow in obedience. Finally, because God has the answers we lack, whenever He speaks, we should listen in silence.

Job 41

"Can you draw out Leviathan with a fishhook?
Or press down his tongue with a cord? . . .
Will he make many supplications to you,
Or will he speak to you soft words?
Will he make a covenant with you?
Will you take him for a servant forever?"   —*Job 41:1, 3–4*

Most of us know how Job's life ends—with repentance and restoration. But what prompted such a repentant spirit in Job? In chapter 41, God reminded Job that He alone can control leviathan (or a crocodile), the most powerful beast in the swamp. Back in Job 40, God demonstrated His sovereignty over behemoth (the hippopotamus), the king of land animals. Having proved His power over the animal kingdom, the Lord proved His power over Job's life. It was as if Job's heavenly Father placed both His mighty hands on Job's shoulders, looked him in the eye, and gave him a firm talking-to. As human parents, we can learn from God's dealings with Job. There are times when nothing works better than placing both of our hands on our small children's shoulders and speaking firmly as we look them in the eye. Our kids need to know we love them enough to exercise loving authority in their lives.

Job 42

"I have heard of You by the hearing of the ear;
But now my eye sees You;
Therefore I retract,
And I repent in dust and ashes."   *—Job 42:5–6*

At the end, Job was the personification of a humble, contrite heart. When faced with the magnificence of God's works, Job repented. Repentance provides two sacrifices God finds pleasure in: a broken spirit and a contrite heart. A contrite heart nurses no grudges, makes no demands, has no expectations, offers no conditions, and anticipates no favors. That's why Job was able to submit to the Lord's will and forgive his friends for their cruelty and judgment. As Christians, we must learn to respond to God as Job did. Remember: everything we own, He owns. Every privilege we enjoy has been granted by His grace. Do we trust God even though we cannot hinder, understand, ignore, or resist His will? As we submit to the Lord, we will build intimate trust in Him . . . and He will use us in amazing ways!

Psalms

Psalm 1

He will be like a tree firmly planted by streams of water,
Which yields its fruit in its season
And its leaf does not wither;
And in whatever he does, he prospers. —*Psalm 1:3*

The descent into fruitlessness doesn't happen all at once. It takes place slowly, one step and one decision at a time. Watch the progression in Psalm 1. Walking day after day in wicked patterns will lead to standing still. And the longer we stand for sin in our lives, the more useless we'll become — like a dried up vine in parched soil. On the other hand, we can live a thriving, fruitful life by following God's ways. And it all begins in our minds. As we read, study, pray, and memorize God's Word, He will begin to renew our minds. As we sink our roots down deep in biblical soil, our actions and attitudes will begin to bear evidence of the Holy Spirit's presence in our lives. Like a strong oak tree, we will be prepared to withstand the trials and temptations that will come our way.

Psalm 2

Do homage to the Son, that He not become angry, and you perish in
*   the way,*
For His wrath may soon be kindled.
How blessed are all who take refuge in Him! —*Psalm 2:12*

It's often best to start a project with the end goal in mind. When a child receives a new puzzle, he or she has the most success by looking at the picture on the box first before arranging the pieces. Likewise, if we want to live a truly successful life, we must live with the end in mind. Psalm 2 gives us the spiritual "box top"—Jesus will one day return to execute judgment on those who have rejected Him and to bless those who have kissed the Son (Psalm 2:12 NIV). As we look around our world, we see war, injustice, misused power, and national leaders who reject Christ's authority. Those of us who have submitted our lives to the Lord should pray for our leaders that they would submit to the Lord Jesus and that they would begin to put together the pieces in their lives to match the picture in Psalm 2.

Psalm 3

*But You, O L*ORD*, are a shield about me,*
My glory, and the One who lifts my head.
*I was crying to the L*ORD *with my voice,*
And He answered me from His holy mountain.   *—Psalm 3:3–4*

When King David's son Absalom gathered a following and usurped the throne of Israel, David fled and went into hiding (2 Samuel 15:13–18). The once-powerful king escaped from Jerusalem, scared for his life. Moreover, the pain of his shattered relationship with Absalom broke his heart. As he hid from his son, David probably wept tears of regret over the years of parental neglect that drove Absalom away. David didn't need only God's protection. David needed God's love and reassuring presence. In this psalm, David acknowledged his enemies but also God's great, sustaining presence. When we're scared and alone, or when we have messed up, how we wish the Lord would show up, wrap His arms around us, and tell us it's going to be okay. Behind our prayers for protection, provision, and guidance is a longing to be near our heavenly Father. Let's trust that He *is* near.

Psalm 4

Tremble, and do not sin;
Meditate in your heart upon your bed, and be still. Selah.
Offer the sacrifices of righteousness,
And trust in the LORD. —Psalm 4:4–5

We don't often associate trembling with worship. Who wants to walk through life with knees knocking? Although King David knew God intimately, prayed transparently, and expected God to answer, David maintained a healthy sense of fear, or awe, of God. He knew that taking God's words lightly often resulted in sin. The Lord desired more than just burnt offerings and sacrifices from Old Testament believers, He demanded obedience (1 Samuel 15:22). God has never been interested in empty-minded religious activity. From Christians today, He doesn't just want church attendance, giving, and serving in the children's ministry. God wants us to submit our lives to His Word. As believers, we must ask ourselves whether we truly revere the Lord enough that it stops us in our tracks when we're tempted. A healthy fear of God will drive us to His Word so we can learn how to honor Him with our actions—to present "sacrifices of righteousness" to Him.

Psalm 5

There is nothing reliable in what they say;
Their inward part is destruction itself.
Their throat is an open grave;
They flatter with their tongue. —Psalm 5:9

A mousetrap may look harmless disguised by a piece of cheese, but it will ensnare a mouse that gets too close. David prayed for

God's protection against the schemes of wicked people. Hiding behind boasting and flattery, they used sweet talk to maintain a harmless appearance while they planned David's destruction in their hearts. God hates pride, and He hates deception — two dispositions that elevate one's own image above God's glory. These two sins precipitated the fall. Satan misrepresented God's command and tempted Adam and Eve to trust their own judgment more than God's. Jesus also condemned pride and deception when He faced the Pharisees. He called them painted tombs filled with death and decay (Matthew 23:27–28). Believers must recognize people who use flattery and lies to destroy others and promote their own name. And we must stay far away!

Psalm 6

I am weary with my sighing;
Every night I make my bed swim,
I dissolve my couch with my tears.
My eye has wasted away with grief;
It has become old because of all my adversaries.   *— Psalm 6:6–7*

After enduring God's chastening rod for some time, David couldn't take any more. He felt so much emotional pain that his body began to ache. David thought his body would give out and believed death would overtake him unless God intervened. He begged God to lift His heavy hand from his frail body. David didn't appeal to his own integrity but based his plea on God's loving and gracious character. Even in the midst of his depression, David was confident that the Lord listened to his weeping and would answer. When we face emotional pain and fear so deep that our bodies wither, do we use unhealthy coping strategies? Or do we turn to God, who can handle our weeping and our whys? Let's take time to examine our relationship with the Lord. Do we interact with Him on a daily basis with intimacy and authenticity as David did?

Psalm 7

O LORD my God, in You I have taken refuge;
Save me from all those who pursue me, and deliver me,
Or he will tear my soul like a lion,
Dragging me away, while there is none to deliver. —Psalm 7:1–2

Cush the Benjamite must have done a number on David. David compared him to a lion that catches its prey with sharp claws and drags it back to his den to devour (Psalm 7:2). Though Cush was, no doubt, unrepentant, murderous, violent, and deceitful, the psalmist trusted in the Lord to deliver him and also to judge Cush. With confidence David declared, "He has dug a pit and hollowed it out, / And has fallen into the hole which he made" (7:15). David turned to God for deliverance and held tight to his own integrity. Humbly, David also asked God to discipline David for his own unknown sin. Many of us have a "Cush" in our lives. Sometimes the Lord allows us to suffer at the hands of others so we will realize our dependence on God. And sometimes God uses an adversary to discipline and refine us. In either situation, we can trust in God's ultimate justice.

Psalm 8

From the mouth of infants and nursing babes You have established
*   strength*
Because of Your adversaries,
To make the enemy and the revengeful cease.   *— Psalm 8:2*

Creation testifies to God's sovereignty and divinity. Only a supremely powerful God could stretch out the heavens, hang the stars on nothing, and hold the universe together with His invisible hands. And no one else but our Lord could design human beings with such intricate beauty and complexity and give us the job of ruling over the earth. That's David's argument in Psalm 8. So how can a God, so clearly majestic, have adversaries who oppose Him (Psalm 8:2)? And how on earth can a newborn baby quiet God's enemies? Anyone who has children can't help but see a little bit of the Lord in that tiny face. Even the staunchest atheist is awestruck when those little lungs belt out their first cry. Even though babies seem so fragile, most whiz through birth, growth spurts, and teething with apparent ease. God has given them amazing strength that reflects His creative hand.

Psalm 9

I will give thanks to the Lord with all my heart;
I will tell of all Your wonders.
I will be glad and exult in You;
I will sing praise to Your name, O Most High.   *— Psalm 9:1–2*

When stress closes in and worry crowds our minds, we often turn to God in urgent prayer. *Lord, help!* King David prayed many urgent prayers. He spent most of his early life running from his enemies. David had many opportunities to worry and even despair of life. But in Psalm 9, we see a pattern for prayer that we, too, can follow. When his enemies closed in, the psalmist fell on his face before the Lord and thanked Him for His imminent deliverance. Next, David chose to be glad in the Lord, even though David wasn't happy about his circumstances. How often do we praise God for His grace in our lives and expect Him to powerfully come to our aid? Let's follow David's example and use God's answers to our urgent prayers as opportunities to thank Him publicly and to give Him credit for His work in our lives.

Psalm 10

You have seen it, for You have beheld mischief and vexation to take it into Your hand.
The unfortunate commits himself to You;
You have been the helper of the orphan.
Break the arm of the wicked and the evildoer,
Seek out his wickedness until You find none. —*Psalm 10:14–15*

When we look around and see evil people exploiting the weak and growing in success, we wonder why God doesn't do anything. Some people come to the conclusion that God is either not all-powerful or not perfectly good. But the psalmist reminds us that although the wicked seem to escape God's justice now, they won't forever. David declared his trust in God's justice and goodness and prayed that He would act to right all wrongs. When we're honest with ourselves, it's sometimes hard to trust God when His justice seems so slow. But the Lord patiently extends grace to those who reject Him, desiring them to repent (2 Peter 2:9). As believers, we must pray for the people in our lives who don't realize their need for God, that the Lord would get their attention through difficult circumstances.

Psalm 11

The Lord is in His holy temple; the Lord's throne is in heaven;
His eyes behold, His eyelids test the sons of men. —*Psalm 11:4*

As David, the future king of Israel, fled from King Saul, he had nowhere to turn. Some of his friends counseled him to flee to the mountains. But David knew that only the Lord, the righteous King of Heaven, could provide refuge. David began his prayer by explaining the problem he faced (Psalm 11:1–3)—the wicked aimed their murderous bows at him. Then he declared his trust in God's protection (11:4–7). Even when David's circumstances and feelings pointed to God's inactivity, David had confidence in the Lord. As modern-day readers of God's Word, we can look back and see that the Lord did protect King David. And we can also read about our Lord Jesus who trusted in the Father when Satan tempted Him and when evil people persecuted Him. Christians stand in a long line of persecuted people who trust in the God of refuge. God does comfort His people when they suffer.

Psalm 12

The words of the Lord are pure words;
As silver tried in a furnace on the earth, refined seven times.
You, O Lord, will keep them;
You will preserve him from this generation forever. —*Psalm 12:6–7*

Each generation seems more godless than the previous one. As time becomes history, God's Word appears to have less and less influence on people's lives. The psalmist lamented that the number of vile people in his life had multiplied. As he conversed with men and women, David noticed more lies and empty sweet talk.

One of the characteristics of the dishonest is that they do not fear God. They view the Lord as far removed from their lives and incapable of judging them. They believe they are above His Law (Psalm 12:4). Like David, we must trust in God's justice. The Bible reminds us that God will defend the poor and needy and one day punish their oppressors (12:5). So when the wicked seem to conduct their schemes without reproach, Christians must remember that God's Word is true — one day His justice will flow like an unending river (Revelation 20:11–15).

Psalm 13

But I have trusted in Your lovingkindness;
My heart shall rejoice in Your salvation.
I will sing to the Lord,
Because He has dealt bountifully with me.   *—Psalm 13:5–6*

"How long, O Lord, will you ignore me? My heart is broken and my body is about to give out. Come quickly, O Lord, and help me!" How many times have we prayed this kind of prayer? Though we plead, sometimes God's answer delays. For years, David sought God's deliverance while he ran from King Saul. Though David nearly capsized in a sea of fear, God did protect David. And not only that, the Lord used Saul's threats to humble David and to prepare him to rule over Israel. When we face devastating sorrow or debilitating fear, let's remember the Lord is trying to draw us to Him and develop our faith. Though He seems far away, our God will never forget or forsake us. Through the pain God allows in our lives, He will develop our maturity and deepen our faith so we can handle the tasks He plans to give us.

Psalm 14

The LORD has looked down from heaven upon the sons of men
To see if there are any who understand,
Who seek after God.
They have all turned aside, together they have become corrupt;
There is no one who does good, not even one.   —Psalm 14:2–3

Look around, and anyone can see that believers and nonbelievers alike are capable of love, desire to do what is right, and
will even sacrifice their own interests for the sake of another.
So when Psalm 14:3 says, "There is no one who does good,
not even one," what does that mean? Because all people have
been made in God's image, we all reflect His goodness to some
extent. But sin has severed every person's relationship with the
Lord. And nothing we do, no matter how noble and praiseworthy, can earn us any favor before God. That's what total
depravity means. Because sin has tarnished every fiber of our
beings, we receive God's favor only through faith in Christ. So
when pride wells up and we start taking credit for the "good"
things we do as Christians, Psalm 14 reminds us that no one
does what is right apart from God's grace.

Psalm 15

O LORD, who may abide in Your tent?
Who may dwell on Your holy hill?
He who walks with integrity, and works righteousness,
And speaks truth in his heart.   —Psalm 15:1–2

Though God's grace covers all our iniquities, it isn't a license to
sin. God demands integrity from His children. But He doesn't
expect believers to tell the truth and do what's right, simply
for the sake of doing it. Pursuing righteousness helps us build

intimacy with our Lord. In Psalm 15, David asks God what it takes to live in fellowship with Him. God considers friends all those who have faith in Christ (John 15:12–15). But how we act—whether we pursue honesty or deceit with our words and resources—affects our relationship with God. Christians should remember that though our eternity in heaven is secure, our relationship with God here on earth can ebb and flow, depending on our obedience to His Word. We would do well to read Psalm 15 regularly and remember that the closer we walk with the Lord, the more the Holy Spirit will produce integrity in us.

Psalm 16

The Lord is the portion of my inheritance and my cup;
You support my lot.
The lines have fallen to me in pleasant places;
Indeed, my heritage is beautiful to me.　　　　—*Psalm 16:5–6*

When our stomachs growl, filling our bellies quickly becomes a top priority. Food is the only remedy for easing our discomfort and restoring our body's energy. Similarly, when worry overwhelms our minds, feasting on God's Word is the only way to peace. King David depended on God for physical and spiritual sustenance. Without God's intervention, David knew he would surely die. In Psalm 16, the psalmist considered God his portion or the source of strength and hope he needed to get through each day. David fixed his mind's eye on God's promises and His salvation even though David's circumstances challenged his faith. Do we, as Christians who have entrusted our eternity to God, trust Him to care for us each day? Is His Word what truly sustains us every day? When our hearts feel empty, let's seek sustenance in our fellowship with God and learn what it means to truly trust in the Lord's provision and protection.

Psalm 17

Keep me as the apple of the eye;
Hide me in the shadow of Your wings.   *—Psalm 17:8*

The pupil controls how much light enters the eye, expanding and contracting depending on how dark or light our environment is. If our pupils aren't working correctly, we will have trouble seeing. Our pupils are so important to the proper functioning of our eyes that God gave us eyelids to protect them. In Psalm 17 when David faced unending attacks by wicked men, he remembered that he was the apple (in Hebrew, *pupil*) of the Lord's eye. David desired God to protect him from the lion-like men who hunted him in the same vigilant, powerful way the Lord might protect His own precious eye. David was confident in his value before the Lord. As Christians, children of God and co-heirs with Jesus Christ, we, too, can develop such a close relationship with the Lord that we can rest in His deep love and intimate care. And we can take all of our sorrows to Him, knowing that He will defend us.

Psalm 18

He delivers me from my enemies;
Surely You lift me above those who rise up against me;
You rescue me from the violent man.
Therefore I will give thanks to You among the nations, O Lord,
And I will sing praises to Your name.   *—Psalm 18:48–49*

Practicing gratitude deepens our faith in God. After years of trusting the Lord to protect him from King Saul, David received yet another answer to his prayers. Immediately, David fell to his knees and thanked the Lord. David loved the Lord, and gave Him credit for providing strength and stability in the face of sure death. David recognized God's intimate involvement in his life. How often do we pray for God's intervention, and then when He answers, forget to thank Him? Rather than attribute answered prayer to coincidence or take the credit ourselves, we must acknowledge God's sovereign, loving work in our lives. The more we depend on God for guidance in large and small decisions, the more we will see His hand. And as we see God working in our lives, may the Holy Spirit prompt us to thank the Lord continually.

Psalm 19

The heavens are telling of the glory of God;
And their expanse is declaring the work of His hands.
Day to day pours forth speech,
And night to night reveals knowledge. — *Psalm 19:1–2*

God makes Himself known in two primary ways — through creation and through His Word. In the first six verses of Psalm 19, David explained that we can discover general truths about God through nature (general revelation). The complexity and beauty of the heavens point to God's power and deity (Romans 1:20). The way the sun rises and sets each day with unswerving consistency points to a faithful God. But general revelation alone doesn't provide all we need for salvation. Psalm 19:7–14 explains that we need God's "special revelation" — the truth about salvation through Christ found in the Bible. David loved God's Law because it has the power to restore, to give wisdom, to impart joy, and to reveal sin. The Bible reveals to us the Person through whom all people can find reconciliation with God. When Christians interact with nonbelievers, we can start with the beauty of creation and help them to see the beauty of God's Word.

Psalm 20

May He grant you your heart's desire
And fulfill all your counsel!
We will sing for joy over your victory,
And in the name of our God we will set up our banners.
May the LORD fulfill all your petitions. —*Psalm 20:4–5*

After God answered David's many prayers for deliverance, David turned around and prayed that God would answer his friends' prayers too. David didn't keep secret the Lord's work in his life. He declared God's faithfulness and asked Him to work just as powerfully in the lives of the people David cared for. And in anticipation of God's intervention, David vowed to rejoice with his friends when the Lord answered. When the Lord works powerfully in our lives, let's use it as an opportunity to tell others about Him. And let's pray that God would grant their hearts' holy desires so that they would put their complete trust in Him. As members of the church pray for each other and rejoice in the Lord's work in their lives, their mutual faith will be strengthened. Then Christians will declare with David, "Some boast in chariots and some in horses, / But we will boast in the name of the LORD, our God" (Psalm 20:7).

Psalm 21

Though they intended evil against You
And devised a plot,
They will not succeed.
For You will make them turn their back;
You will aim with Your bowstrings at their faces. —*Psalm 21:11–12*

Some people hate God and make it their aim to slander His name. Often they hate believers, too, because they represent the

Lord. King David experienced the attack of rebellious, godless men, but he trusted in God's justice. David knew that when King Saul sought to kill him and when Absalom usurped his throne, they had revolted against the Lord. God had appointed David as king, and any effort to dethrone him amounted to disobedience to God. At the heart of rebellion against God is pride — placing oneself above the Lord. Though God-haters intimidated David, he knew that God would ultimately deal with God's enemies (Psalm 21:12). When Christians receive threats and persecution from others because of our faith in Christ, we shouldn't fear. And we shouldn't be surprised. Our Lord Jesus warned us that those who hate Him will take out their anger on His followers (John 15:18 – 19). But He will eventually judge.

Psalm 22

Posterity will serve Him;
It will be told of the Lord to the coming generation.
They will come and will declare His righteousness
To a people who will be born, that He has performed it.
— Psalm 22:30 – 31

As Jesus completed His task on the cross, the darkness closed in. Sweat and blood dripped from His forehead. He who had never known loneliness felt completely abandoned by His Father. So He called out, "My God, My God, why have You forsaken Me?" (Mark 15:34). Many years earlier King David had prayed this same prayer. As his enemies closed in and his life hung in the balance, David felt forsaken by God. David cried out to his heavenly Father, hoping to hear His voice in return. In Psalm 22, David vacillated between crying for mercy and praising God for His deliverance. But David ended with confidence that future generations would know God's righteousness. And ultimately, when Jesus quoted David's words on the cross, He reminded people that, though God seemed silent, He was displaying His righteousness to the whole world and generations to come. May we use our suffering to point others to the One who suffered on our behalf.

Psalm 23

Even though I walk through the valley of the shadow of death,
I fear no evil, for You are with me;
Your rod and Your staff, they comfort me.   —*Psalm 23:4–5*

When the road before King David twisted behind trees and dipped into dark valleys, he didn't fear. He drew on his experience as a shepherd when he had used a rod and staff to care for his sheep. A rod was a club used to chase away wolves, and a staff was a long stick with a hook used to pull sheep out of thickets and holes. David counted on his heavenly Shepherd to protect him from his enemies and rescue him from danger. Christians today must trust that same Shepherd. Because we are human beings with finite knowledge, the uncertain path before us causes fear. We need a guide who not only knows the destination but can shield us on the journey. Our Good Shepherd, Jesus Christ, knows and loves His sheep. So when dark valleys and unknown roads stretch out before us, we can walk with confidence.

Psalm 24

Lift up your heads, O gates,
And be lifted up, O ancient doors,
That the King of glory may come in!   —*Psalm 24:7*

Jerusalem had long been an enemy stronghold. But finally, with God's help, David conquered it and established the City of

David—the future home of God's temple. Because the temple had not yet been built, David put the ark of the covenant in a tent and led the people in worship (2 Samuel 6:17–19). To celebrate the entry of the ark, which represented God's presence, David called on personified gates and doors to lift their heads up and joyously receive the King of Glory. This triumphal entry of God's presence into Jerusalem in David's day pointed forward to the triumphal entry of the God-Man into Jerusalem before His crucifixion and resurrection (Matthew 21:6–9). And believers today can look forward to the reign of the King of Glory from the New Jerusalem, with gates that will remain open forever (Revelation 21:25–27).

Psalm 25

Redeem Israel, O God,
Out of all his troubles.   *—Psalm 25:22*

Suffering often causes us to turn inward and forget others, and self-pity inevitably leads to selfishness. But in Psalm 25, which starts as an individual lament psalm, David ends by praying that God would save Israel. Throughout this song, David asks for deliverance and guidance, confesses his sin, thanks the Lord for forgiveness, and reflects on God's goodness. Though he started with an eye on his cruel enemies, David kept his focus on God's character. And this focus on the Lord enabled David to pray for God's grace not just in his own life, but in the lives of his people. Likewise, when Christians focus on God's attributes and thank Him for His mercy, we will begin to pray that others would experience God's goodness too. Just as David turned his precarious situation into an opportunity to pray for Israel, Christ-followers who hurt should remember to pray for members of His global church who are suffering.

Psalm 26

Examine me, O Lord, and try me;
Test my mind and my heart.
For Your lovingkindness is before my eyes,
And I have walked in Your truth. —*Psalm 26:2–3*

When we are mistreated, it's easy to doubt God's love. And when we doubt God's love, we lose our rudder in life and eventually drift into sin. So how did David stay on course when his enemies victimized him? David resolved to keep his eyes fixed on God's "lovingkindness"—His covenant faithfulness. The Lord revealed this central attribute in Exodus 34 in response to Moses's desire to see God's glory. The Lord passed before Moses and declared His name: "The Lord, the Lord God, compassionate and gracious, slow to anger, and abounding in lovingkindness and truth" (Exodus 34:6). With this picture of God in mind, David sought to honor Him in times of struggle and victory. With laser focus, Christians must zero in on God's love when we are mistreated. Let's read and reread Exodus 34:6 and surround ourselves with like-minded believers who will encourage us when our circumstances and feelings tempt us to doubt.

Psalm 27

For my father and my mother have forsaken me,
But the Lord will take me up. —*Psalm 27:10*

Though his enemies tracked his every step and plotted to kill him, David lamented an even more depressing reality. David's own father and mother had forsaken him, leaving him feeling totally alone and afraid. Though his earthly parents had failed him, David's heavenly Father would never leave him. With that in mind, David started and ended this psalm by praising God for His sovereign care, which drove away David's fear. David also trusted that his Lord would allow him to dwell in God's house — in intimate fellowship with Him — for eternity. Those who have been deserted by their mother or father know what it means to cling to the Lord when fear closes in. And, though many believers have not been abandoned by their parents, we have all experienced loss in our relationships. In those painful times, let's seek out intimate fellowship with our Father and build relationships with those who have been abandoned.

Psalm 28

Save Your people and bless Your inheritance;
Be their shepherd also, and carry them forever.   — Psalm 28:9

When a sheep strays from the flock into dangerous territory where wolves prowl, the shepherd will leave the flock to find the lost sheep. If that stubborn sheep strays from the flock repeatedly, a good shepherd will scoop up the sheep, break its leg, and carry it back into the fold. The shepherd doesn't hurt the sheep because he is angry, but because he wants to train his sheep to stay close. So when Israel faced godless foes, David prayed that the Good Shepherd would carry the people of Israel and save them from harm. But many times throughout history, God's people strayed, and He had to discipline them to teach them to stay close to Him. Likewise, though Christians have a secure eternal destiny, sometimes we stray from our Lord and expose ourselves to danger and temptation. May we respond to His loving discipline and learn to stay close to Him.

Psalm 29

"The LORD sat as King at the flood;
Yes, the LORD sits as King forever."   —*Psalm 29:10*

While Israel's neighbors attributed natural phenomena to pagan gods, David gave credit to the Lord. When lightning flashed and thunder shook the earth, the psalmist heard the powerful voice of God. David called his contemporaries to worship the creator God who alone sends rain to water the earth and causes the sun to rise and warm the land. David pictured the world as God's temple and every living thing as a worshiper. The psalmist recalled the Lord's eternal justice and power displayed in the flood that drowned the whole earth in Noah's day. And David reminds Christians that the God who revealed His majesty in the flood and who makes His power known in the weather will work just as powerfully in our lives today. Let's ask the Lord to display His power in the problems we are facing. And let's expect Jesus, who calmed the raging storm, to work in our lives.

Psalm 30

You have turned for me my mourning into dancing;
You have loosed my sackcloth and girded me with gladness.
                                          —*Psalm 30:11*

Each time we fail, we have an opportunity to develop humility. Whenever God disciplines His children, it is for the purpose of restoring us to closer fellowship with Him. King David failed often and, therefore, had many chances to develop humility and intimacy with the Lord. Prosperity had caused David to trust in himself, which ultimately led to sin (Psalm 30:6). As David prepared to dedicate the tent in which the ark of the covenant resided, he reflected on God's grace in his life. And he rejoiced (Psalm 30:11–12). Believers today should be aware that prosperity will tempt us to trust in ourselves. When we begin to rely on ourselves instead of God, let's approach Him and ask for forgiveness. God disciplines us, not to shame or depress us but to remind us of our need for Him. Christians who have received God's lavish forgiveness are more willing to extend it to others.

Psalm 31

Be gracious to me, O Lord, for I am in distress;
My eye is wasted away from grief, my soul and my body also.
For my life is spent with sorrow
And my years with sighing;
My strength has failed because of my iniquity,
And my body has wasted away.   *—Psalm 31:9–10*

Human beings aren't just souls trapped in bodies. God created us with bodies and souls that work together to make us who we are. When physical pain or disease debilitates us, we often feel its effects in our souls in the form of depression or anxiety. And when secret sin and fear plague our souls, the symptoms usually extend to our bodies. When David felt distress in his soul because of his many foes and grief because of his own sin, David's body "wasted away." Sorrow sapped his physical strength. But the psalmist believed in the Lord's forgiveness so David begged God to intervene and to bless him. We, too, can ask God to bless us and to restore our health, body and soul. And we must remember that unconfessed sin and unexposed misery in our souls will manifest themselves in our physical health. So let's seek God's grace and the support of others.

Psalm 32

Do not be as the horse or as the mule which have no understanding,
Whose trappings include bit and bridle to hold them in check,
Otherwise they will not come near to you. —Psalm 32:9

David wrote Psalm 32 in order to impart insight he had learned firsthand. David's body had started to waste away because of his unconfessed sin. Many sleepless nights and worry-plagued days had taken their toll. Though David had stubbornly kept certain areas of his life hidden, he finally confessed his sin to the Lord. After receiving God's forgiveness, David felt total relief. He wrote this song to celebrate the Lord's amazing grace and to encourage all people to confess their sins to the Lord sooner rather than later. David had experienced personally the consequences of stubbornly covering over his sin. Christians who think they can hide their sin from God are on a collision course with pain. God sees everything. In His grace, God sometimes uses the physical ramifications of a tormented conscience to drive us to Him. Thankfully, through Christ, God stands ready to forgive and extend grace (1 John 1:9).

Psalm 33

Sing to Him a new song;
Play skillfully with a shout of joy. —Psalm 33:3

What kind of God can scoop up the sea with His hands and stack the waters in a pile? And what kind of Lord reigns with perfect justice and infinite kindness? Surely, He is worthy of our worship! And not just worship of any kind but skilled, joyful praise. When the psalmist thought of God's character, he grabbed his lyre and his harp and wrote a new worship song.

Each time the Lord intervened in his life, David learned more about God's character. And each new divine facet David discovered made him want to sing for joy! When we experience different aspects of God's nature — His sovereignty, kindness, or justice — do we thank Him by worshiping Him in song? Do we come up with imaginative ways to praise Him? Even if we don't consider ourselves "the creative type," we were made for worship. Our creator God deserves our innovative and skilled worship!

Psalm 34

This poor man cried, and the LORD heard him
And saved him out of all his troubles.
The angel of the LORD encamps around those who fear Him,
And rescues them.   *—Psalm 34:6–7*

While David was on the run from King Saul, he entered Gath in the land of the Philistines. When he got there, David feared that the king of Gath would recognize him and kill him. So David escaped by pretending to be insane, scratching on doors and allowing saliva to run down his beard (1 Samuel 21:10–15). Then, he cried out to the Lord for protection and God answered. Though terror had gotten the best of him, David realized that running from fear only made matters worse. He learned that turning to the God who commands armies of angels is more trustworthy than his own efforts to protect himself (Psalm 34:6–7). When fear paralyzes us, we often think that we must do something to alleviate it. And often our attempts at self-preservation only increase our uncertainty. Christians must remember that the Lord will send His angels to help us in the midst of our trials.

Psalm 35

Let them be like chaff before the wind,
With the angel of the LORD driving them on.
Let their way be dark and slippery,
With the angel of the LORD pursuing them.   *—Psalm 35:5–6*

David's enemies were not limited to Saul, Absalom, and other human beings. As the Lord's anointed and chosen ruler over Israel, David had spiritual foes too. Satan and his army of demons surely attacked David with arrows of fear, swords of despair, and false messages that God had abandoned him. But in this psalm, he thanked God for salvation and prayed that the "Angel of the Lord" would overpower and drive away his adversaries. Who was the Angel of the Lord? In many Old Testament passages, the Angel of the Lord may refer to the pre-incarnate Christ, the second person of the Trinity. In Ephesians 6:12–13, the apostle Paul reminded Christians that though we may fight against people who don't like us and who want to see us fail, our battle is ultimately against Satan and his evil army. Let's depend on help from Jesus Christ who, through His death and resurrection, has disarmed our adversaries (Colossians 2:15).

Psalm 36

In their own eyes they flatter themselves
too much to detect or hate their sin.   *—Psalm 36:2 (NIV)*

The psalmist roots sin in the absence of the fear of the Lord. The wicked person doubts God's justice, disbelieving that his or her actions will be punished. The godless individual justifies immoral actions in order to quiet the faint inner voice of conscience. Surely if his or her conscience were allowed to speak, it would voice its hatred about his or her evil exploits. All human beings were created in the image of God. Though God's likeness is marred due to our sin, human beings have the capacity to know good and evil. Just as the vast universe, majestic mountains, and mysterious sea point to God's unparalleled power, the inner voice of conscience points to God's perfect justice. But, even believers who have been indwelled with the Holy Spirit can quiet His voice through our consistent rebellion. Have we flattered ourselves and justified sin in our lives? If so, we must return to the Lord.

Psalm 37

Delight yourself in the LORD;
And He will give you the desires of your heart. —*Psalm 37:4*

Our God-given emotions provide a window into our souls. When disappointment strikes, what emotions do we feel? More specifically, what do we feel *about God* in those dark moments? Many Christians quote "Delight yourself in the LORD and He will give you the desires of your heart," but do we really believe it? And do our desires reflect a lifestyle of delight in God? In Psalm 37, David helps believers to root their deepest desires in a vibrant, joyful relationship with the Lord. If our longings stem from worry or jealousy, God probably won't honor them (Psalm 37:1). If they stem from impatience or anger, our yearnings likely don't come from Him (37:7–8). But if our recurrent prayers revolve around pursuing fellowship with the Lord and seeking to further His glory, He will likely answer them. Let's examine the desires God has given us according to Psalm 37.

Psalm 38

For Your arrows have sunk deep into me,
And Your hand has pressed down on me.   —*Psalm 38:2*

The discipline of the Lord can feel like arrows puncturing our flesh or a heavy hand crushing all of our bones. At times it can feel as though God has abandoned us, and as though we have out-sinned the Lord's ability to forgive. But David knew better. Though his body ached under God's discipline, the psalmist trusted that the Lord would soon extend grace and healing. David proclaimed, "I hope in You, O Lord; / You will answer, O Lord my God" (Psalm 38:15). What do we think about God when we have sinned? Do we believe what the Bible says about His grace when we *feel* as though He has forsaken us? Even when God allows our friends and family to turn away from us because of our transgression, do we still turn to Him for comfort? Let's learn to develop a relationship with the Lord like David's, which survives our own failure.

Psalm 39

"Turn Your gaze away from me, that I may smile again
Before I depart and am no more."   —*Psalm 39:13*

David acknowledged the transient nature of his life. As quickly as a breath, he would one day pass away. So the psalmist didn't want to spend his last fleeting days as the object of the Lord's censure. He mentioned the short life of man five times in this brief psalm. It seemed to him that God's heavy hand would press on him until the day he died. David begged the Lord to relent. But he couldn't convince God to stop His discipline short of its intended purpose — to refine David's character as gold purified in the furnace. Christians who have experienced God's discipline know how penetrating His gaze can be. Even though we know His grace and forgiveness outweigh our sin, it sometimes feels like God's displeasure will last forever. But it won't. The Lord will restore joy and gladness when His discipline has achieved its goal — to make us more like Christ.

Psalm 40

Then I said, "Behold, I come;
In the scroll of the book it is written of me.
I delight to do Your will, O my God;
Your Law is within my heart." — *Psalm 40:7–8*

God had delivered the psalmist from external enemies like King Saul and Absalom and from the internal enemies of adultery and pride. David had experienced God's fatherly discipline, His endless grace, and His sovereign protection. So as the anointed king of Israel, David vowed not only to obey the Mosaic Law but to treasure it in his heart and give himself as a sacrifice to God. But David wasn't the only king who treasured God's Word and sacrificed His life in obedience. The Lord Jesus fulfilled the entire Law and became the means by which His followers could receive grace and eternal life (Hebrews 10:5–10). With this in mind, Christians must remember what Christ has rescued us from — our past, present, and future sins, as well as our efforts to achieve righteousness through any human-made standards. Now we must present ourselves as living, obedient sacrifices that God can use to bring others to Him (Romans 12:1–2).

Psalm 41

Even my close friend in whom I trusted,
Who ate my bread,
Has lifted up his heel against me. —Psalm 41:9

In this Psalm, David struggled with the infidelity of human beings. One of David's close friends whom he trusted had betrayed him. But the stinging pain of such disloyalty drove him to the Lord, in whom there is perfect faithfulness. David believed that God would not only defend him but also judge his deceptive friend. The Lord Jesus also knows what it feels like to be betrayed by a close friend. After Judas succumbed to Satan's prompting, he led the authorities to Jesus. Though as God, Christ had control over His life and death; as a man, He felt the sting of betrayal. So when the book of Hebrews says that our Great High Priest can sympathize with our weaknesses and struggles, let's trust it (Hebrews 4:15–16). And when we experience betrayal, let's run to Christ to find grace and comfort and then turn to comfort others with the Holy Spirit He has given us.

Psalm 42

O my God, my soul is in despair within me;
Therefore I remember You from the land of the Jordan
And the peaks of Hermon, from Mount Mizar. —Psalm 42:6

Despair opens a gaping wound within our hearts, and we search desperately for a salve to soothe our souls. When pushed into a similar corner, the psalmist sought God. Many of us may be surprised at where the psalmist found the Almighty. While in the agony of despair, the psalmist remembered God "from the land of Jordan / And the peaks of Hermon, from Mount Mizar" (Psalm 42:6). In other words, the answer to despair was in the concrete blessing of the Promised Land that he saw all around him—the flowing waters of the Jordan River and the soaring peaks of Israel's northern mountains. Today we have a tendency to spiritualize our problems and their solutions. And, while we do need to be attentive to the immaterial side of the equation, we need also remember that God's physical creation stands as a powerful testimony to His power and provision—comforting truths as we tend our wounds in the frigid wasteland of despair.

Psalm 43

O send out Your light and Your truth, let them lead me;
Let them bring me to Your holy hill
And to Your dwelling places.   —Psalm 43:3

The psalmist had been tormented by an unjust person. Though he asked God for vindication and defense (Psalm 43:1), the psalmist felt cut off and alone (43:2), as if he were in a place of terrifying darkness. So he asked God to send the light of deliverance into this disturbing situation. He also wanted to be led by God's "truth"—to see an illustration of God's faithfulness, assuring him that the Lord would be true to Himself and His word. God's guidance through difficulty and His faithfulness to His Word would prompt the psalmist to offer God praise on God's "holy hill"—a metaphor for the Old Testament place of worship, the Temple Mount. When injustice strikes and we find ourselves in a dark and lonely place, we need a guide. God is the only One who can see us through the darkness of despair and bring us back to a place of joy and gratitude.

Psalm 44

Our heart has not turned back,
And our steps have not deviated from Your way,
Yet You have crushed us in a place of jackals
And covered us with the shadow of death. —*Psalm 44:18–19*

Many believers strive to be faithful to God in every area of their lives. But sometimes, with that pursuit of faithfulness comes the expectation that all things will go our way and that we will be kept from the harsh realities of pain and death. However, God makes no such promises. Though we follow Him down that narrow path, we will experience, at times, personal illnesses, community downturns, and the deaths of those close to us. When the psalmist spoke of God crushing the people "in a place of jackals" and covering them "with the shadow of death," he referred to the lair of an animal that often scavenges for food and is most active in those dark hours between sunset and sunrise. We can expect hardship to cross our paths. But we, like the psalmist, must also remember to call upon God, for He alone is our help; He alone is our hope of redemption (Psalm 44:26).

Psalm 45

Your throne, O God, is forever and ever;
A scepter of uprightness is the scepter of Your kingdom. —*Psalm 45:6*

While God's throne will certainly last forever, the psalmist actually is taking the unusual step of referring to the Davidic king in divine terms (Psalm 45:6). As the earthly representative of God's people, the Davidic king stood in a deity-like relationship with the nation of Israel. As such, the king would have been expected to uphold God's standard of righteousness, modeling that standard for the kingdom under his governance. As a descendant of David, Jesus stands as the perfect Davidic king, and He will rule His kingdom with perfect righteousness upon His return to earth. Because Jesus is our supreme example of conduct in life, His upright leadership should influence how we carry ourselves in our own leadership positions. We may not be kings and queens, but we lead others in a host of ways — a team at the office, a family in the home, a class at church. May we each strive for uprightness in our dealings with others.

Psalm 46

God is our refuge and strength,
A very present help in trouble.
Therefore we will not fear, though the earth should change
And though the mountains slip into the heart of the sea.
—Psalm 46:1–2

Fear grips and guides many in these uncertain times. The twentieth century celebrated the progress of humanity resulting from our own rational and scientific giftedness. The twenty-first century has seen that dream fail in disastrous conflicts and loss of true community. Today's people see little we can rely upon. This modern-day condition creates a perfect opportunity for truths such as we see in Psalm 46. When our world is in upheaval, we have Someone we can rely upon. God is still in heaven. He has retained His power and strength. And He remains deeply engaged with His creation. Because our refuge is in God, the One to whom we can run in terrible times, we can set fear aside. Let us not be afraid of governments or disease or neighbors. Instead, just as God is a strong refuge, let us be a people of strength, a people who offer refuge to others in a world turned upside down.

Psalm 47

O clap your hands, all peoples;
Shout to God with the voice of joy. . . .
He chooses our inheritance for us,
The glory of Jacob whom He loves. —*Psalm 47:1, 4*

Who's in control of our lives? Many in our world have bought the lie of self-determination. We believe that due to certain freedoms, we are in control of our own lives. In this scenario, God comes along for the ride, offering help whenever we feel we need it. The psalmist, however, presents a much different picture of the relationship between God and humanity. God determines our destination. For those who follow Jesus, God has planned a glorious inheritance. This should lead us, the psalmist says, to clap our hands and shout for joy—typical human expressions of celebration and gratitude. When we humbly adopt this perspective of God's sovereignty and cast off the destructive impulse of self-determination, we acknowledge that God alone can lead us to that glorious, heavenly inheritance. Constantly seeking to determine our own way will lead only to frustration, conflict, and, ultimately, destruction.

Psalm 48

*Great is the L*ORD*, and greatly to be praised,*
In the city of our God, His holy mountain. —*Psalm 48:1*

Throughout history, God has always made it a point to seek out His people and dwell with them. In the first moments after Adam's fall, God sought the first man in the garden (Genesis 3:8–9). God also visited Abraham, Moses, and others throughout history. When the Israelites had settled down in the Promised Land under the leadership of David, God lodged with the people in Jerusalem (2 Samuel 6:12–17), which was located on a mountain. And since the resurrection and ascension of Jesus, God has stayed with His followers through the indwelling presence of the Holy Spirit. The borders of the old "city of God" have expanded to include people from all over the world. God now makes His dwelling not just in a single temple, but in the temples of our bodies (1 Corinthians 6:19–20). May we always be confident of His presence with us, at every moment, wherever we are.

Psalm 49

No man can by any means redeem his brother
Or give to God a ransom for him—
For the redemption of his soul is costly,
And he should cease trying forever.   *—Psalm 49:7–8*

Wealth creates innumerable opportunities to do good in the world. For instance, the unfortunate reality of modern-day slavery sometimes can be rectified by paying the high cost to redeem a person from his or her owner. However, while this approach might work in reference to physical slavery, it has no hope in reference to spiritual slavery. The Bible makes clear that human beings are in bondage to sin without God's gracious deliverance (Romans 5:17–18). The psalmist invoked this idea of spiritual redemption to illustrate the dark underside of riches. Money can buy a great deal, but it cannot buy spiritual redemption. We have to recognize the real limitations of riches—homes and possessions crumble, and even we will eventually perish. Psalm 49 encourages us to be people of "understanding" in the right use of money, rather than fools who glory in financial accomplishments instead of glorying in God (Psalm 49:13, 18–20).

Psalm 50

These things you have done and I kept silence;
You thought that I was just like you;
I will reprove you and state the case in order before your eyes.

—Psalm 50:21

Wickedness has a way of skewing our perception of reality. When caught up in some undesirable habit or behavior, we find many different ways to convince ourselves of the rightness of our course. We can become so deeply enmeshed in sinful behaviors and attitudes that we might even begin to believe that God somehow approves of our wickedness. This was the condition of the Israelites, a condition the psalmist sought to bring to their attention. We must not mistake God's silence in the face of our evil deeds as His approval. God in His goodness will never approve of wickedness. Instead, God expects that we will order our ways aright (Psalm 50:23), that we will give and not steal, endure and not stray. Only then will we see clearly that our great, powerful, and gracious God guides the way toward a life of goodness, not wickedness.

Psalm 51

Against You, You only, I have sinned
And done what is evil in Your sight,
So that You are justified when You speak
And blameless when You judge.

—Psalm 51:4

David sinned. As king, he used his power to take advantage of Bathsheba and have her husband killed. Upon being confronted by the prophet Nathan, David humbled himself before God, calling for the grace of purification that so many of us long for after we have fallen. And while David grievously wronged Bathsheba and her husband, Uriah, ultimately the king sinned against God. Psalm 51 presents sin as an evil deed in God's sight (Psalm 51:4), as well as a condition that plagued David from birth (51:5). We see here that sin creates significant problems in our relationships and circumstances. But more than that, David's response to his failure reminds us that our sin places us in opposition to God. And when we find ourselves there, we should respond as David did: ask for grace and purification, that we may come to God with a "broken and contrite heart" (51:17).

Psalm 52

But as for me, I am like a green olive tree in the house of God;
I trust in the lovingkindness of God forever and ever. —Psalm 52:8

When young David fled from the murderous King Saul, the future king received assistance from Ahimelech the priest. One of Saul's servants, Doeg the Edomite, witnessed the incident and reported it to Saul. Enraged that anyone would help David, the king ordered Doeg to kill eighty-five priests. David's psalm, which accuses a "mighty man" of boasting in evil and devising destruction (Psalm 52:1), works as a response to Doeg's evil deeds as well as a comment on the wicked. Those who do evil face spiritual death, and David contrasts them with the company of the righteous—those who trust in God's *chesed*, or loving-kindness. When we succumb to doing evil in stressful circumstances, we place ourselves at risk, not only from the immediate consequences of our actions but also from our resulting broken fellowship with God. Instead, like David, we should illustrate our trust in God's loving-kindness by keeping to the narrow way of righteousness.

Psalm 53

The fool has said in his heart, "There is no God,"
They are corrupt, and have committed abominable injustice;
There is no one who does good.   *—Psalm 53:1*

When he referred to the fool who says, "There is no God" (Psalm 53:1), David didn't have in mind ancient atheists. Everyone in the ancient world believed in some god. The "fool" of Psalm 53 stands for a wicked person. David focused in this psalm on actions rather than beliefs. The wicked act as if they have no God. The wicked live as self-determining individuals, rather than as people under authority. The wicked, therefore, commit injustices against their fellow human beings. Our beliefs about God impact our deeds, just as our deeds impact our beliefs about God. When we believe that we can live on our own, apart from God's direction for us, we court wickedness and its terrible results. When believers regularly practice sin, Christian beliefs that once may have been clear and true become muddied and false. We must take care, therefore, to protect our minds and our deeds, that we might fulfill Jesus's ideal for us (Matthew 22:37).

Psalm 54

Behold, God is my helper;
The Lord is the sustainer of my soul.   *—Psalm 54:4*

David had retreated into the wilderness of Maon (1 Samuel 23:24–25), a desolate area west of the Dead Sea, where remaining hidden and avoiding Saul's pursuit were paramount. However, a local people called the Ziphites reported David's location to Saul. David wrote this psalm in remembrance of that time, when strangers rose up against him and violent men were on his trail (Psalm 54:3). At this moment in David's life, his desperation was palpable. Only God could save him. Only God would sustain his life. Like David, many of us have found ourselves in desperate situations with few options and even fewer answers. While we would never wish for such moments in our lives, we recognize that they provide an opportunity to exercise our trust in God as our defender and sustainer. When our circumstances signal desperation, we should always strive to recognize God's power in our lives.

Psalm 55

Cast your burden upon the Lord and He will sustain you;
He will never allow the righteous to be shaken. —Psalm 55:22

For some, prayer consists of dictating terms to God, as if He were a personal valet. However, this psalm of David gives a clearer picture of prayer. The psalmist encourages us to cast upon God our "burdens"—which means, literally, what He has given us. As circumstances occur in our lives, we in turn should entreat God about those same circumstances. Our casting of burdens upon God places us in a submissive position to Him. Asking God to help us with things too heavy to bear on our own reveals our weakness and His strength. When we do cast those cares upon God, we can expect that He will sustain us through our difficult circumstances. He promises that He will keep those who follow Him—the "righteous"—from being shaken. By trusting in God to handle the greatest and even the least of our cares, we can expect to find the greatest security we have ever known.

Psalm 56

In God, whose word I praise,
In God I have put my trust;
I shall not be afraid.
What can mere man do to me?   —*Psalm 56:4*

Everything changes when we recognize the fundamental difference between God and humanity. He is the Creator. We are the creation. As such, God possesses strength and wisdom far beyond our own. And yet, our habits lead us either to cower or to lash out when we feel threatened by other people. Our impulsive action reveals a lack of awareness about or appreciation for the distinction between God and humanity. God's great power and wisdom should bring peace to those who follow Him. In turn, we should not get caught up worrying over the machinations of evil men. None of this means we are exempt from pain in this life. Pain may, in fact, visit us often. But, we can proceed with courage instead of fear, knowing that our praiseworthy and trustworthy God remains in power, willing and able to care for His people and propel us to the kinds of lives He has in mind for us.

Psalm 57

My soul is among lions;
I must lie among those who breathe forth fire,
Even the sons of men, whose teeth are spears and arrows
And their tongue a sharp sword.   —*Psalm 57:4*

The Hebrew word Psalm 57 uses for "soul" can also be translated "breath," which creates a potent physical image of David's proximity to danger. His very breath among the lions, David could not make a false move. In such a critical circumstance,

David's request for divine mercy that he might find safety in the shadow of God's ample wing takes on life and death implications (Psalm 57:1). The psalm takes us back to Saul's pursuit of David, while the king-to-be hid in a cave with no obvious means of escape. We sometimes find ourselves in places of danger — physical, yes, but spiritual danger as well. Wicked people and temptations lurk around the corners of our lives, out of sight for the moment but close at hand. In those dangerous places, may we also call upon God's mercy, that He might spread the goodness of His glory throughout the earth (57:5).

Psalm 58

[The wicked] have venom like the venom of a serpent;
Like a deaf cobra that stops up its ear,
So that it does not hear the voice of charmers,
Or a skillful caster of spells.   —*Psalm 58:4 – 5*

Wickedness estranges us from God. Though believers falter in our struggle against sin, we ultimately desire lives of purity. In contrast, this psalm compares people who do not follow the true God to cobras that purposely ignore the voice of their charmers (Psalm 58:4 – 5). God woos His creation with a beautiful song, only to be ignored by those who seek their own pleasure and comfort. The end of such wickedness is judgment, a truth that gives the righteous confidence that God does, in fact, care about their plight (58:11). God will not rid the world of evil prior to Christ's return, but the very hope of that promise and its ultimate fulfillment should lead Christians to cast off wickedness in favor of service to God. For when believers toy with wickedness, we are, in essence, courting the life of a serpent in the tradition of that most wicked and cursed of creatures (Genesis 3:1, 14 – 15).

Psalm 59

For no guilt of mine, they run and set themselves against me.
Arouse Yourself to help me, and see! —*Psalm 59:4*

David wrote this psalm in the context of Saul's men pursuing and hoping to capture or murder him. On the run and with feelings such as any man might have, David wanted to see these pursuers punished. No doubt he would have happily taken up the mantle himself. However, David restrained himself out of respect for God's anointed, King Saul. Instead of lashing out at his pursuers with his sword, David called upon God to do the work for him. David expressed to God his hope that his enemies would be judged. David's restraint regarding his enemies should still be instructive for us today. Many of us decide to take on ourselves the task of judgment, forgetting that judgment is ultimately God's business, not ours (James 4:12). We would be better off in God's eyes and in the eyes of our neighbors if we modeled David's restraint.

Psalm 60

O give us help against the adversary,
For deliverance by man is in vain.
Through God we shall do valiantly,
And it is He who will tread down our adversaries.

—*Psalm 60:11–12*

As followers of Christ, we recognized our need for God's empowering grace at the time of salvation. We now rely on Him in our day-to-day lives, understanding that we can live out His ideal for us only with His gracious assistance. Does relying on

God's grace imply that we sit around and do nothing? Quite the opposite, in fact. When the psalmist called upon God for help, he understood that God would do His work through the army's efforts in battle. We cannot expect to deliver ourselves from the deepest difficulties that life presents. God desires to work on our behalf, to deliver us from terrible circumstances, and to empower us to act well in the midst of trying times. Therefore, when we call upon God, we look to Him to act and we give Him the credit for deliverance, but we must also recognize our responsibility to live in accordance with His desires.

Psalm 61

So I will sing praise to Your name forever,
That I may pay my vows day by day.   *—Psalm 61:8*

Psalm 61 recounts David's confidence that God would give him a long reign as king over Israel and, by extension, a long life as well. David concluded the psalm with a commitment to sing praises to God forever. The rest of his life would be an act of praise to God. Therefore, David followed up that commitment in anticipation of the results: he would offer "vows day by day" (Psalm 61:8). God's blessing in David's life had changed David—the king meant to live a life of daily devotion to God precisely because David so appreciated God's blessing in his life. In the same way, when we begin to grasp God's good work in our lives, we can respond to God as David did—by making and, more importantly, fulfilling vows. As we encounter God's blessing, what kinds of commitments can we make to God, purely out of gratefulness?

Psalm 62

My soul, wait in silence for God only,
For my hope is from Him. —*Psalm 62:5*

In this day of devices and electronics, we have largely lost the habit of living with silence. But in the modern-day world of nearly constant noise, the value of silence has only increased. Taking advantage of quiet for a particular time each day can dramatically change the way we see the world. As it did for David, a time of silence can turn our attention toward God, so that we can better appreciate His work in our lives. In addition, taking time out of our day to consider God in silence lessens our distractions, helps us focus on what's important, and if we approach the time prayerfully, can dramatically alter our relationships with others. David waited on God in silence, and it reminded the king of the source of his hope. In the same way, as we take opportunities for silence in our lives, we better embody the hope that God has given us.

Psalm 63

My soul is satisfied as with marrow and fatness,
And my mouth offers praises with joyful lips. —*Psalm 63:5*

David invoked the elements of a luxurious feast—marrow and fatness—to describe his own satisfaction with God's presence in his life. This fulfilled state led David to praise God with joy. Our God fully satisfies at the deepest levels of human life. Like the culture around us, Christians can easily get caught up in a lifestyle of always looking for the next thing. This can lead to a deep sense of dissatisfaction with our lives and people around us. When we are dissatisfied and discontent, we lack the abiding joy of those who have given themselves completely to the service and praise of God. We spend too much of our time looking for created things to appease our discontent, when in reality, only the Creator can fill that void. Let us each follow David's example, finding our satisfaction in God and reaping the rewards of joy.

Psalm 64

Hear my voice, O God, in my complaint;
Preserve my life from dread of the enemy. —Psalm 64:1

The Bible presents a long history of faithful individuals complaining to God about their circumstances. Abraham expressed his discontent about the destruction of Sodom and Gomorrah (Genesis 18:16 – 33). Job complained about the suffering that had come into his own life (Job 16:6 – 22). And in this psalm, David complained to God about the enemies that had come upon him. Expressing discontent or laments to God has never been wrong when the individual refuses to lay the blame for evil at God's feet. Instead, God seems to welcome and encourage such honest communication from the faithful. When we approach God in prayer, we have the opportunity to welcome Him into the difficulties of our lives. We, like David, can trust that God will hear our prayers. And just as He humored Abraham, answered Job, and delivered David on numerous occasions, we know that God will respond in the way He chooses—which is always best.

Psalm 65

You visit the earth and cause it to overflow;
You greatly enrich it;
The stream of God is full of water;
You prepare their grain, for thus You prepare the earth.

—Psalm 65:9

God cares for His creation. He provides for it. He nourishes it. David celebrated God's abundant blessings in the forms of flowing water, softened ground, and bountiful crops (Psalm 65:10–11). God's love for His creation does not stop at mere affirmation. He expresses His care for the world by tending to its needs. Just as God loves and enriches the earth, so should we. Many contemporary Christians are so focused on the spiritual realm that we fail to consider the physical needs around us. Taking good care of the material creation that God has blessed us with often fails to become a priority for even the most devout believers. But we can see in God's command to Adam to tend the garden of Eden that part of our purpose as humans is to care for the land. An active concern for the physical world around us should characterize God's people around the globe.

Psalm 66

Come and see the works of God,
Who is awesome in His deeds toward the sons of men.
He turned the sea into dry land;
They passed through the river on foot;
There let us rejoice in Him!

—Psalm 66:5–6

This psalm of praise to God uses as its centerpiece God's great act of deliverance when He brought the Hebrews through the Red Sea. God's presence at the Red Sea was unmistakable—He made

Himself known in a concrete fashion through His actions. The psalmist used this singular event in Israel's history as the grounds for himself (Psalm 66:11), for Israel (66:10), and for people of all nations (66:8) to offer praise to God. All people—individuals, communities, nations—should rejoice in God as they remember His great and mighty works. And the Lord makes this easy for us by making Himself known in such distinctive ways. Let us all take comfort in the multitude of ways God has made Himself known in history, and how those concrete acts provide forthright knowledge of the Lord. That God has made Himself known by working in our world should give us confidence that He also works in our individual lives.

Psalm 67

God blesses us,
That all the ends of the earth may fear Him.   *—Psalm 67:7*

God's blessings witness to others, drawing people of all nations to Himself. God is the Lord over all people. Some consider Him as a nationalistic God of only one people, Israel. However, the Scriptures declare Him as accessible to all. The psalmist calls for God's grace so that people everywhere may experience salvation (Psalm 67:2). God's gracious intervention in the world—such as the bountiful harvests He provides (67:6)—is evidence that He will ultimately serve as guide to people of all nations (67:4). Because God's blessings serve to reveal God's grace to people of all kinds, then believers today should make it a priority to make that grace known far and wide. The signs of His presence in and His care for the world are numerous and bright. Believers simply need to point them out, giving others the opportunity to know the joy of salvation (67:4).

Psalm 68

God makes a home for the lonely;
He leads out the prisoners into prosperity,
Only the rebellious dwell in a parched land. —*Psalm 68:6*

Our separation from other people can cause us to feel confined. We, then, should not be surprised at David's associating the lonely with the prisoner. Where do we turn when loneliness brings us low? How can we break free of the isolation that leaves us feeling surrounded by seemingly impenetrable walls? We can cling to God's promise in Psalm 68. God can break through all barriers. He roots the prisoner in prosperous land. And He makes homes for the lonely far more substantial than mere walls and roofs. God creates true community. His vision for all of us involves the presence of people and connection. He knows that we need others in our lives. And just as we need others, so others need us. We need to search out the lonely in our communities and bring them into our homes that they, too, might break free from their prisons of sin and isolation and experience the joy of the Lord.

Psalm 69

I have sunk in deep mire, and there is no foothold;
I have come into deep waters, and a flood overflows me.
                                                    —*Psalm 69:2*

When we look for heroes and saints among biblical prophets, kings, and apostles, we run the risk of forgetting their frailties. Many of them did great things, but they had weaknesses too. Psalm 69 records David's depression. He expressed feeling as though he were drowning with nothing solid in his life with which to find stability. Water, so often a blessing in Scripture, became for David, during this time, a symbol of danger to his very life. Many inside and outside the church today struggle with the kinds of feelings David recorded in this psalm. We weep endless tears. We feel pressure from selfish individuals who don't have our best interests at heart. And we just feel like we are sinking. David called on God for help, recognizing the ultimate source of deliverance. God may use a variety of means to deliver us, but we, like David, can rely on God's positive work in our lives.

Psalm 70

Let those be turned back because of their shame
Who say, "Aha, aha!"   —Psalm 70:3

Tearing down and criticizing others has risen to near-epidemic levels in today's climate. Increasingly, people feel the need and the freedom to make their critical opinions known, often with little consideration for the individuals implicated. As David penned this psalm, he had in mind those types of people, the kind that love to tear down and to take pleasure in the pain of others. David prayed that these individuals would be pressed into changing their ways by their guilty consciences. This type of healthy, appropriate shame over wrongdoing has lessened in contemporary culture, and we are reaping the consequences of lax morals and lowered standards. As Christians, we can reestablish the value of "godly sorrow" (2 Corinthians 7:10) by responding well when we ourselves stumble. Healthy shame over sinning against others brings with it a necessary dose of humility and the impulse to make those relationships right. May we each have the courage to be ashamed over our missteps.

Psalm 71

I have become a marvel to many,
For You are my strong refuge.
　　　　　　　　　　　　　　　　　—*Psalm 71:7*

We show ourselves marvelous when we take refuge in the Lord. In other words, the psalmist recognized that others would be captivated when God's people found in Him refuge from their troubles. The great human temptation always leans toward finding our own way and shaking off the guidance and assistance of others. When we take this posture, we act as if the Lord cannot deliver us or that He is too busy to save, which was the position the psalmist's enemies took as they peppered him with insults and abuse (Psalm 71:10–11). But as the psalmist found security in the Lord despite the attacks, people around him began to take notice. Often the best statements we make for God are spoken through actions rather than through words. Therefore, we turn to the Lord during difficult times not only for personal comfort, but to make Him known and attractive to those around us.

Psalm 72

And let all kings bow down before him,
All nations serve him.
　　　　　　　　　　　　　　　　　—*Psalm 72:11*

God is the greatest over all kings. In His complete love for righteousness, justice, and peace, the Lord reveals Himself to be far above any human leader in history. None have loved their people and embraced the good as God has. And yet, we often treat the Lord as if He were a close friend or confidant, instead of our king, our ruler, our master. Many today have forgotten what it means to live under authority, to obey despite our wishes and desires that point in a different direction. Instead, we embrace the so-called wisdom that says our desire for an object or end justifies our pursuit. Solomon's psalm reminds us that fulfilling our desires must come after our service to and worship of the true King of the universe. When we live under the authority of the world's ultimate King, we humble ourselves before Him and come away with a better idea of who He is and who we are.

Psalm 73

Surely God is good to Israel,
To those who are pure in heart!
But as for me, my feet came close to stumbling,
My steps had almost slipped. — *Psalm 73:1–2*

As one of Israel's choir leaders, Asaph outwardly led God's people in worship. Inwardly, however, Asaph had a problem — one he had to keep to himself so he wouldn't lead Israel astray (Psalm 73:15). Asaph struggled with jealousy. He looked around at godless people and saw that they were wealthy even though they shook their fists at God. Then the choir leader looked at his own life of obedience and strife and wondered if he had kept his heart pure in vain. How did this psalmist overcome bitterness toward the prosperity of the wicked and ultimately toward God? Asaph entered God's sanctuary (73:17). And how can believers today overcome envy? The same way. We must spend time with God, let His Word reorient our outlooks, and begin to view life from an eternal perspective. Though the godless seem carefree now, one day they will face the justice of the Lord.

Psalm 74

Remember Your congregation, which You have purchased of old,
Which You have redeemed to be the tribe of Your inheritance;
And this Mount Zion, where You have dwelt. —Psalm 74:2

When the Lord made the covenant with Israel on Mount Sinai, He promised to bless His people as long as they obeyed Him. But if they disobeyed, God said, He would curse them. In 586 BC, the Lord used the great Babylonian Empire to discipline His people. As the Babylonians invaded, they destroyed Jerusalem and God's temple. This may have been what the psalmist Asaph lamented in Psalm 74. As he passed by the Lord's house, the smoldering ruins and gloating enemies broke the choir leader's heart, and he begged God to remember His chosen people—to relent and to restore them. As Christians, we too experience God's discipline. When we do, like the psalmist, we can appeal to the Lord based on His promises. Through Christ, God has saved us and will never abandon us. So let's pursue obedience, and when we fail, let's ask God to bring restoration when His discipline has reached its end.

Psalm 75

"I said to the boastful, 'Do not boast,'
And to the wicked, 'Do not lift up the horn;
Do not lift up your horn on high,
Do not speak with insolent pride.'" —Psalm 75:4–5

If we work hard and exert time and effort to achieve a goal, what's wrong with tooting our own horns and taking a little credit? That's what the godless thought in Asaph's day. They relied on their own strength and pointed to their great power when they achieved success. They forgot that all of their abilities came from the Lord. When they neglected gratitude, pride took over their hearts, and God hates pride. The Lord has promised that those who boast in their own strength will be humbled — He will break their horns (Psalm 75:10). When we succeed, there's nothing wrong with acknowledging our own gifts and talents, but when we forget that they originate with God, we begin to slide down the slippery slope of pride. Let's guard our hearts against boasting and use the success God gives us to proclaim His strength and not our own.

Psalm 76

His tabernacle is in Salem;
His dwelling place also is in Zion.
There He broke the flaming arrows,
The shield and the sword and the weapons of war. —*Psalm 76:2–3*

In Psalm 76, Asaph described a precarious situation akin to the extraordinary actions God took to protect His dwelling place in Isaiah 37. When Jerusalem faced the threat of attack from Assyria, the most powerful nation on earth, Jerusalem's inhabitants trembled in fear. But in response to King Hezekiah's prayer, the Lord of Heavenly Hosts defended His city (Isaiah 37:36–38). God defeated Israel's enemy miraculously by sending His angel to kill 185,000 Assyrian troops as they slept. When we face insurmountable obstacles and fear closes in, let's remember that the Lord has limitless resources. And not only *can* He answer our desperate prayers miraculously; He *wants* to come to our aid because He loves us. Whether the bills are due and there's no money to pay them or a relationship is broken beyond hope, our God can work powerfully and sovereignly to answer our prayers. When He does, let's give Him the credit.

Psalm 77

I shall remember the deeds of the LORD*;*
Surely I will remember Your wonders of old.
I will meditate on all Your work
And muse on Your deeds.   —*Psalm 77:11–12*

Asaph tossed and turned in his bed, feeling alone and abandoned. But instead of letting depression take over, Asaph confessed his anxiety to the Lord. And instead of letting loneliness get the best of him, Asaph drew near to God, admitting his doubt to the Lord and turning his mind to God's character. Though the Lord seemed to have abandoned His people, Asaph recalled God's consistent record of faithfulness. How often the Almighty had stepped in when it seemed hopeless. The same God who parted the Red Sea and rescued His people from Egypt (Psalm 77:16–20) works powerfully in Christians' lives today. When doubt creeps into our minds, like Asaph, let's draw near to the Lord, confess our anxiety to Him, and turn our attention to meditating on His faithfulness in our lives and throughout history as revealed in His Word.

Psalm 78

For He established a testimony in Jacob
And appointed a law in Israel,
Which He commanded our fathers
That they should teach them to their children.   —*Psalm 78:5*

Asaph recalled the history of God's people, from their escape from Egypt to God's provision of the shepherd-king David. The choir leader reminded Israel of God's persistent grace in spite of their grumbling and disobedience. When the Lord delivered Israel from Egypt, He provided manna to eat, water from a rock, and protection from enemies. God had consistently provided for Israel, yet the nation had complained and chased idols. Before we condemn Israel for forgetting God's grace, we must each ask ourselves: *Do I do the same thing?* How often do we close our eyes to God's work in our lives and complain because things aren't going our way? How often do we forget to thank Him for our salvation and for the grace that cost Jesus so much? Let's take time each day to recall God's consistent record of faithfulness in our lives and in His Word, and let's honor His grace with obedience.

Psalm 79

Help us, O God of our salvation, for the glory of Your name;
And deliver us and forgive our sins for Your name's sake.

—Psalm 79:9

The psalmist knew that the Lord desired to use Israel — both by blessing the nation and by disciplining it — to draw *all* nations to Himself. So after a foreign nation had destroyed Israel and left its victims in the streets to be eaten by birds and beasts, Asaph appealed to God and begged for grace. The psalmist called on the Lord, not based on Israel's repentance or good deeds but on God's good name. The psalmist worried that if the Lord waited too long to restore Israel, the surrounding nations would think Yahweh had forgotten His people and conclude that He wasn't a faithful, covenant-keeping God. God still works through

Christians to make His great name and reputation known. The question is, do our prayers for help, deliverance, and provision take into consideration God's reputation? When we pray, we must ask: *Are my prayers selfish, or do I want God's glory to be displayed through His work in my life?*

Psalm 80

O God of hosts, turn again now, we beseech You;
Look down from heaven and see, and take care of this vine,
Even the shoot which Your right hand has planted,
And on the son whom You have strengthened for Yourself.
—Psalm 80:14–15

Psalm 80 pictures God as the cosmic gardener and Israel as His vine. The Lord prepared the ground and planted Israel in the Promised Land and then built a wall of protection around the nation. Under His care, Israel grew strong and spread its branches and blessing from the Euphrates River to the Mediterranean Sea. But the nation soon forgot about its divine vinedresser and sought sustenance from other gods. In response, God broke down Israel's wall and allowed foreigners to invade until His people repented and relied on Him. In Psalm 80, Asaph prayed that the Lord would stop disciplining Israel and that He would again take care of His vine. Christians today are also like a vine, but we can only bring blessing to others if we're grafted into the true vine, Jesus Christ (John 15). As believers, we must trust our heavenly Father, the vinedresser, and learn to abide in Christ in order to bear fruit.

Psalm 81

"You called in trouble and I rescued you;
I answered you in the hiding place of thunder;
I proved you at the waters of Meribah."   —*Psalm 81:7*

When Israel observed the Feast of Tabernacles each year to commemorate their deliverance from Egypt and God's provision in the wilderness (Leviticus 23:34), they not only celebrated the parted sea and miraculous meals. They also recalled their great test at Meribah. In Exodus 17:1–7, God told His exhausted people to stop and rest from their journey, but the place He told them to stop had no water. When their thirst got the best of them, they didn't call out to God; they grumbled against Moses. Though they failed the test, the Lord graciously provided water from the rock. God still gives believers opportunities to put our faith into action. These tests strengthen our trust in the Lord and prove His ability to come through for us, whether we pass or fail. Each time the Lord tests us, we should write the experience down so we can recall God's faithfulness to help us face the next test.

Psalm 82

God takes His stand in His own congregation;
He judges in the midst of the rulers.   —*Psalm 82:1*

The impartial exercise of authority is one of the greatest proofs of godliness. Those who use their God-given power to uplift the downtrodden, provide for the poor, and defend the weak show submission to the Lord. But those who abuse power by showing partiality to the rich and influential will be judged by the true Judge. The psalmist called such abusers in Israel to account and asked God to mete out punishment. With no respect for the Lord, these judges had used their authority unfairly, so much so that the foundations of society had become unstable. Most of us don't have that kind of power. However, we all exercise some measure of authority. Parents "rule" over kids. Bosses have power over employees. Pastors exercise spiritual authority. Daily, we use our positions, skills, and influence with either wisdom or pride. As Christians, may we always show impartiality, defend the afflicted, and operate with wisdom that comes from fearing the Lord.

Psalm 83

O God, do not remain quiet;
Do not be silent and, O God, do not be still.　　　　*—Psalm 83:1*

Sometimes God seems silent, distant, and immovable. We pray, and it seems like He isn't listening. But He is. God always hears the prayers of His people. Asaph wrote his final psalm, thinking on Israel's enemies, who were planning violent attacks and seeking Israel's destruction amidst God's apparent silence (Psalm 83:6–12). For Asaph, God's stillness must have felt almost as dreadful as the enemy's threats. But the psalmist remained faithful, beseeching the Almighty to move, to step into His people's distress and defend them. Most Christians have felt like the Lord is too busy to hear our prayers and too slow to act. When difficult circumstances and sadness increase our anxiety, how can we handle God's apparent silence? We can search Scripture for God's words for our situation. And we can choose to believe that not only does our Lord hear our prayers, but He loves us and is in complete control.

Psalm 84

My soul longed and even yearned for the courts of the LORD;
My heart and my flesh sing for joy to the living God.   —Psalm 84:2

Believers are foreigners longing for a homeland. So how do we find comfort in this world that is not our home? Psalm 84 reminds us that we must pursue the Lord's presence, which in the Old Testament was symbolized by the temple. Though only the Levitical priests could enter God's temple, all of His people could worship in the courts of His temple. And as they praised God in His courts, they developed intimacy with Him. As believers in Christ, the Lord is with us. The Holy Spirit indwells and empowers us and gives us companionship when we're lonely. He pushes us into community with other believers, which provides comfort. Let's examine our hearts first to be sure we really do long for the Lord's presence in our lives. And then, while we wait for our eternal homecoming, let's draw near to Him through His Word, His Spirit, and His people.

Psalm 85

Lovingkindness and truth have met together;
Righteousness and peace have kissed each other.   —Psalm 85:10

If Israel sinned against the Lord and worshiped the idols of neighboring nations, God swore to punish them by sending them into captivity (Deuteronomy 28:41). But He also promised to bring them back to their land when they repented (30:1–5). In Psalm 85, the psalmist celebrated the fulfillment of that promise—Israel's restoration. Based on the biblical account of Israel's history, the pattern of God's discipline and restoration points to His faithfulness and righteousness. God's loving-kindness meant that no matter how disobedient Israel was, God would always keep His covenant to give the nation the Promised Land. And because He is righteous, God wouldn't tolerate Israel's sin. When God's people understood these aspects of His character, they acted according to His truth and lived in peace. The same principle rings true for us today. Through Jesus, Christians have received peace with God and the promise of everlasting life. Therefore, let's live each day according to God's truth.

Psalm 86

Teach me Your way, O LORD;
I will walk in Your truth;
Unite my heart to fear Your name. —*Psalm 86:11*

More than anything, King David wanted to please the Lord. David was, after all, a man after God's own heart (Acts 13:22). Yet even with these credentials, the shepherd-king knew that he had no hope of honoring God unless the Lord helped him. So first, David asked God to teach him His way. As the king read God's Law, he prayed for the wisdom to understand and the ability to obey. Next, David entreated God to unite his heart in the fear of the Lord. Like David, without God's help, we'll never truly honor Him. And if we have divided hearts, we won't be able to walk the straight path of obedience. As Jesus taught, we can't have two masters (Matthew 6:24). If we couple the love of anything else with our love of God, our divided hearts will lead us away from the Lord.

Psalm 87

Then those who sing as well as those who play the flutes shall say,
"All my springs of joy are in you."   —*Psalm 87:7*

God chose Zion (Jerusalem) as the place where He would commune with His people. The Lord's presence rested in the temple there as His people gathered to worship Him. The Israelites, who had received the promise of a future prophet (Deuteronomy 18:15–19) and an eternal king (2 Samuel 7:8–16), looked forward to a time yet to come when God will reign from Zion and subdue all their enemies (Isaiah 2:1–4). At just the thought of future Zion, the Israelites felt joy. Their joy will one day be *complete* when Jesus Christ reigns from Zion during the millennium (Revelation 14:1–5). Christians today experience God's presence through the indwelling Holy Spirit and through meeting together as the body of Christ. These give us joy, but like the Israelites, our joy will be made complete in the future. Though disappointments steal our joy now, one day the Lord will reign from the New Jerusalem, and we will worship Him forever with joyful singing (21:10–27).

Psalm 88

O Lord, the God of my salvation,
I have cried out by day and in the night before You.   —*Psalm 88:1*

When the Almighty is silent, do we search for answers elsewhere, or do we wait for Him to speak? Psalm 88 paints a picture of perfect submission and patient endurance in the midst of intense suffering. The psalmist began this powerful prayer with a foundational theological statement: God alone can provide physical, emotional, and spiritual salvation. Though the psalmist's circumstances seemed to contradict this truth, he clung with a tight grip to the God of his salvation. How do we as believers in Jesus Christ react when God doesn't answer our prayers? Do we begin to redefine God's attributes because we don't feel His love? Or do we reaffirm what we know to be true about Him and wait patiently for His sovereign timing? Regardless the pain, suffering, poverty, anxiety, or death that may close in, we must cling to the God of our salvation, rely on His Word, and surround ourselves with others who will encourage our faith.

Psalm 89

"I have made a covenant with My chosen;
I have sworn to David My servant,
I will establish your seed forever
And build up your throne to all generations."   —*Psalm 89:3–4*

Ethan, one of King David's Levitical singers (1 Chronicles 15:16–17), wrote Psalm 89. In this prayer, Ethan interceded for David and asked the Lord to remain faithful to the covenant He had made with the king. For thirty-seven verses, Ethan recalled the words of God's covenant with David (2 Samuel 7:8–16) and praised the Lord for His loyal love. Then in the next thirteen verses, the psalmist lamented God's apparent rejection of David when his enemies seemed to have the upper hand. Ethan's intercessory prayer for King David teaches us to pray God's Word on behalf of others. The apostle Paul recorded many other prayers that we can pray for ourselves and for others. When we do, we can have confidence that God will answer. And like Ethan, we can end our intercessions with a proclamation of trust in God's sovereign will: "Blessed be the Lord forever! / Amen and Amen" (Psalm 89:52).

Psalm 90

You turn man back into dust
And say, "Return, O children of men."   —*Psalm 90:3*

Human beings possess life only because we have received it as a gift from the Almighty. The language of Psalm 90 evokes memories of the creation narrative. The Hebrew word *adam*—translated here as "men"—specifically recalls the Genesis account, while the mention of returning to dust brings to mind God's death curse upon Adam (Genesis 3:19). The psalmist—Moses in this case—wanted us to remember the powerful way that God sustains our lives, a reminder which should result in our taking our lives seriously and attempting to live each of our days with wisdom (Psalm 90:12). Do you measure out your days, seeking the best and wisest approach for each one? Such an approach will set us apart as God's people and prepare us for the many good works God has in store for us. It all begins with a proper recognition of God's power over life and death.

Psalm 91

He will call upon Me, and I will answer him;
I will be with him in trouble;
I will rescue him and honor him.   —*Psalm 91:15*

Over and over, the Psalms point out individuals seeking—and finding—shelter in God, our refuge. The sheer repetition of the theme can lead us to an appreciation of God's reliability. Psalm 91 takes up this theme once again, and here, the psalm includes a response from the Lord that highlights His presence in our times of trouble. In this verse, God takes His promise even further, vowing to "honor" the one who calls upon the Lord.

The Hebrew term translated "honor" is the same one often used to describe God's glory (Isaiah 40:5). God's plans for His people involve not just rescue, but also glorification (Romans 8:30). We who call upon the name of the Lord for salvation and help have a great hope! We will not always be beset by troubles. Like the psalmist, we can take God at His word—He will glorify us.

Psalm 92

A senseless man has no knowledge,
Nor does a stupid man understand this:
That when the wicked sprouted up like grass
And all who did iniquity flourished,
It was only that they might be destroyed forevermore.

—Psalm 92:6–7

By way of inspired Scripture, God offers a clear definition of a stupid person in Psalm 92. Stupidity in biblical terms has nothing to do with skills in mathematics or knowledge of literature. The stupid and the senseless are those who do not understand the appointed end of the wicked. Regardless what they may enjoy on earth, evildoers will receive judgment. Failing to recognize the gravity of this coming judgment, the stupid person goes ahead with life as if nothing is wrong. Most of us have noticed wickedness in our world and feel distraught when evil succeeds. And we should! When evil stops disturbing us, we must ask ourselves if we've strayed into the territory of the stupid and senseless. When our senses dull to evil, we risk inviting it into our lives in ever-increasing ways. Therefore, let's trust judgment to our Lord and remain vigilant against the presence of evil in our lives by showing the proper level of concern for those who practice evil in our communities.

Psalm 93

Your throne is established from of old;
You are from everlasting.   —*Psalm 93:2*

The psalmist pictured the Lord on high, distinct from humanity, as the One who reigns, who possesses strength, and who keeps the world stable. This kingly figure has been on the throne "from of old," for He is "from everlasting." In other words, almighty God began His reign as king when He created the earth. He could do that, in part, because He is eternal. God's eternality can seem like a distant concept that has little to do with day-to-day life. However, the fact that God alone has always existed provides Him with an authority over creation that extends to everything and everyone. We live in a world where humans have largely conferred ultimate authority upon ourselves. But such a world can lead only to chaos. Therefore, we should fall in line under the authority of the eternal God, the only One who can grant eternal life.

Psalm 94

Blessed is the man whom You chasten, O Lord,
And whom You teach out of Your law.   —*Psalm 94:12*

How often do we run from discipline? We prefer to go our own way, in our own time, by our own means. However, the only possible rescue from our innate foolishness comes as a result of God's chastening. In Psalm 94, the psalmist spoke to the evil people who had risen against God's people, urging them to pay attention to the Lord—their rebuke from on high would come. In contrast, the psalmist called the disciplined man "blessed."

God's discipline is good, even if our experience of it is unpleasant. We rarely, if ever, yearn for someone to discipline us, and usually, we don't even like to discipline ourselves. Yet, the wise among us come to appreciate the Lord's discipline, if not during the rebuke, then at least after (Psalm 95:15). On the other hand, when God's discipline visits the foolish, their response reveals the wickedness deep within them.

Psalm 95

For He is our God,
And we are the people of His pasture and the sheep of His hand.
Today, if you would hear His voice,
Do not harden your hearts, as at Meribah,
As in the day of Massah in the wilderness.   *—Psalm 95:7–8*

When God's people quarreled with Moses over lack of water in the desert, they expressed their wish to still be living in Egypt. At that moment, they preferred bondage rather than the alternative: trusting God to provide for their needs. Psalm 95 encourages God's people to remember the lesson learned that day in the wilderness and see God in the same way that sheep regard their shepherd. Just as the shepherd provides pasture and guidance for his sheep, so does God provide for His people. And just as sheep tend to wander from the path and resist their shepherd in stubbornness, so can we easily wander from God's way and choose not to listen to His voice. Being attentive to God's voice involves reading His Word, memorizing it, and hearing it taught through a local church. When we make God's Word a regular part of our lives, we have a better sensitivity to what God's expects of us.

Psalm 96

Let the field exult, and all that is in it.
Then all the trees of the forest will sing for joy
Before the LORD, for He is coming,
For He is coming to judge the earth.
He will judge the world in righteousness
And the peoples in His faithfulness. —*Psalm 96:12–13*

All creation rejoices at the prospect of God's coming judgment. But why? The apostle Paul taught us that creation has been groaning since Adam's fall (Romans 8:22). Paul pictured the created world as waiting for God's intervention, looking forward to a time when all would finally be put to rights. And while judgment brings negative consequences to some, others look with joyful anticipation to a time when righteousness rules the day. With righteousness at its peak in this post-judgment era to come, life will proceed as God originally planned. As we look forward to this time of righteousness in the future, we should intentionally live out righteousness in our lives now. It isn't enough simply to wait for God to come and make everything right. The Lord wants us to embrace righteousness in the here and now (6:12–13).

Psalm 97

Clouds and thick darkness surround Him;
Righteousness and justice are the foundation of His throne.
—*Psalm 97:2*

In our expressions of faith, we tend to emphasize the accessibility of God—the reality that He has made Himself known to us through His Son, Jesus Christ. When we see Jesus, we see the

Father (John 14:9). And yet, there remains around the Father a great deal of mystery, for to have a complete knowledge of God would be to contain Him. Psalm 97 reveals this truth with its imagery of "clouds and thick darkness" (Psalm 97:2). For us, who are finite and limited, God the Father, who is infinite and unlimited, remains mysterious in certain ways. The mystery that surrounds the Lord extends to His attributes—perfect righteousness and justice also carry with them a sense of mystery this side of heaven. Therefore, as we seek to live out God's ideals on earth, let us never believe we have arrived. We press on along the mysterious path toward fully embodying God's best for us.

Psalm 98

O sing to the LORD a new song,
For He has done wonderful things,
His right hand and His holy arm have gained the victory for Him.
—Psalm 98:1

The basis of the psalmist's praise in Psalm 98 lies in the "wonderful things" that God has done (Psalm 98:1). Describing God's deeds as "wonderful" evokes images of events that are beyond human capabilities. As clear expressions of His care for His creation, God's deeds inspire wonder and astonishment. God's people have faith in a miraculous God, One whose works cannot be explained by scientific formulas or mere reason. We live in a cynical age in which wonder gets pushed aside in favor of harsh truths and hard realities, and a shortage of wonder leads to vacuous worship. Part of the problem is our lack of expectation. We don't expect to be filled with wonder at God's works; therefore, we never marvel at those works. However, if we change our expectations, we'll give ourselves ever-greater opportunities to wonder . . . and to praise God with gusto.

Psalm 99

Moses and Aaron were among His priests,
And Samuel was among those who called on His name;
They called upon the LORD and He answered them. —*Psalm 99:6*

As a record of humanity's history, Scripture contains numerous instances of human failure. However, we also find in the Bible many positive examples—those men and women who, despite their failures, understood something important about the life of faith. The psalmist invoked specific Israelites who interceded for God's people—the term *priests* being used more broadly to refer to intercessors. Why highlight these particular men, though? The lives of Moses, Aaron, and Samuel show that God is indeed a God who reveals Himself among His people. Consider yourself as one of God's people. Will you be seen as evidence of God's working in the world? Or will you contribute to others' belief that God's work has ended? In the tradition of Old Testament saints, let's commit to interceding for God's people so by our actions we might be the conduits through which God makes Himself known in the world.

Psalm 100

Shout joyfully to the LORD, all the earth. —*Psalm 100:1*

As followers of Christ, we understand that joy should characterize our lives and our dealings with others. Yet, our reason for that joy sometimes gets lost. Yes, we rejoice over our salvation, but Psalm 100 adds to the picture, showing us that joy is not something we conjure up ourselves. Instead, joy builds within us as we acknowledge and react to the truth that not only has God saved us, He has made us and we are His people (Psalm 100:3). In other words, we have entered into relationship with Him! The reality of that relationship—God's acknowledgment that He has not left us alone in this world—touches one of the deepest human needs. We were all made for community—with God and His people. Finding love, concern, and comfort in the presence of others fulfills us like no other experience. Therefore, as we remember our God-given relationships—with God and with others—we respond with joyful worship.

Psalm 101

I will set no worthless thing before my eyes;
I hate the work of those who fall away;
It shall not fasten its grip on me.   *—Psalm 101:3*

David's commitment to living an upright life was deeply connected to the people around him. He saw those in his community who cared little for the things of God, and he rejected their work and their lifestyles (Psalm 101:3). Further, as king, he had the power of the government on his side to silence slanderers and ban the arrogant (101:5). David also saw and drew inspiration from those in his land who did pursue a proper way of life (101:6). In short, *all* of David's community dealings flowed from his refusal to set worthless things before his eyes and his vow to keep his gaze on the blameless. David didn't want to find himself caught in the grip of evil, and the impact of his commitment teaches an important lesson. Making and keeping a commitment to avoid evil has the potential to dramatically alter much more than our individual lives. It can change our communities as well.

Psalm 102

"Even they will perish, but You endure;
And all of them will wear out like a garment;
Like clothing You will change them and they will be changed."
— Psalm 102:26

As Christians, we look forward to the day when our unchanging, eternal God will finally and fully redeem His creation. Since the fall, God has been in the business of changing that creation, redeeming it from the consequences that sin has wrought. The psalmist affirmed God's endurance by contrasting it with the creation that will ultimately pass away. Specifically, Psalm 102 employs the image of a garment wearing out and being changed. The affirmation is significant. Yes, creation groans under the weight of humanity's collective sin. Yes, our natural resources melt away as corporations, governments, and individuals misuse the land, sea, and air. But there is hope. God, who is unchanging, will turn the tide and change this planet for the better. Rather than contribute to the downward spiral of death, let's find ourselves working on the side of renewal and life, on the side of our unchanging, world-changing God.

Psalm 103

As far as the east is from the west,
So far has He removed our transgressions from us. *— Psalm 103:12*

We all sin. And yet, when God saves us, He considers us separate from our sin. Upon being saved, we no longer need to be sold out to our selfish desires. Instead, God has linked us to Himself so that we might better live out His ideal for humanity. God's removal of sin's penalty from those who follow Him changes our lives! No longer need we wrack ourselves with guilt over past failings. Neither are we bound to continue courting sin. With God's power on our side, we can successfully resist the call of sin. Before salvation, guilt drove our actions, and we willingly submitted to temptation, but as believers, we're called to a better life, one that seeks to honor God and others before ourselves. Let's express our thanks to God by living according to the picture of Psalm 103:12—as people far removed from transgression.

Psalm 104

He causes the grass to grow for the cattle,
And vegetation for the labor of man,
So that he may bring forth food from the earth. —Psalm 104:14

God loves life. The created world testifies to this love. He gave life to the world, and He continues to give and support it every moment of every day. From the driest desert to the lushest rainforest, God's world teems with living creatures. *Everywhere* the earth sustains some kind of life, and that fact should encourage all who have eyes to see. But perceiving that life—and appreciating it—can be a challenge in our modern-day world of concrete, asphalt, and glass. Worse, we often let our eyes fixate on death instead—tsunamis, explosions, disease, and terror. Those events are certainly present in our world and bring with them darkness and faltered hope. Yet, the presence of renewing and continuing life shines all the more in the midst of that darkness. So, watch the grass grow. See the trees drink. Look at God's world and be encouraged.

Psalm 105

Until the time that his word came to pass,
The word of the LORD tested him. —*Psalm 105:19*

To highlight the Lord's deliverance and direction of His people, the psalmist recalled Joseph's plight of slavery and imprisonment. But, Psalm 105 reminds us, before deliverance came testing. God often operates in this fashion, testing those who follow Him before finally removing them from their difficulties or changing their circumstances. Just as the Lord tested Joseph, so, too, does He test us. Often, we see negative circumstances as evidence of God's punishment for some hazy sin. But while God does discipline His children, He also tests His faithful followers. Such tests force us to pose pointed questions to ourselves: *Where does my strength lie? Does God truly love me? Can God deliver?* The opportunity to grapple with such questions, as well as shine God's light into the world through our faithfulness in spite of hardship, reveals times of testing as more than times of pain . . . they're also moments of opportunity.

Psalm 106

Therefore the anger of the LORD was kindled against His people
And He abhorred His inheritance. . . .
And He remembered His covenant for their sake,
And relented according to the greatness of His lovingkindness.
—*Psalm 106:40, 45*

Israel's history has been well-documented. Chosen specially by God, the nation failed in its obedience. The Lord was faithful to them, but they were not faithful to Him. Repeated failure over the course of centuries led to God's anger and abhorrence

(Psalm 106:40). In modern times, we most often think of abhorrence — or hatred — in starkly emotional terms. However, God's abhorrence is less about emotion and more about rejection — a reality made clear by Israel and Judah's forcible ejection from the Promised Land. God rejected His people, but not forever. He remembered His covenant and saved them from the exile. We too might find ourselves in a kind of exile — removed from God, church, and family in any number of ways for any number of reasons. We can know, however, that God is characterized by loving-kindness and grace; He is ever calling and inviting us to join Him. The Lord's rejection is never forever for those who love Him.

Psalm 107

He pours contempt upon princes
And makes them wander in a pathless waste.
But He sets the needy securely on high away from affliction,
And makes his families like a flock.   *—Psalm 107:40–41*

In this world, we tend to honor the exalted — the political leaders, the sports heroes, the celebrities — those who seem to transcend the normal grind that most of us endure. In honoring those "higher-ups," we often ignore the lowly — the poor, the needy, and the diseased. However, God measures people in a different fashion — those great in the world's eyes will "wander in a pathless waste," while the lowly will find a place of security "away from affliction" (Psalm 107:40–41). God provides protection for the most vulnerable of society, and as His followers, we should model our lives after this value. And yet, we invariably spend more time following the glitter of the world's "bright lights" than we do offering a helping hand to those on the lowest rungs of society's ladder. In pursuit of holiness, may we shift our attention to those most in need of our help.

Psalm 108

Be exalted, O God, above the heavens,
And Your glory above all the earth. — *Psalm 108:5*

God dwells beyond the heavens and the earth. The psalmist, David here, used the context of praise to acknowledge this fact. The God who dwells above all life and creation warranted the king's praise, even as Israel faced impending danger. The true God transcends our sufferings and difficulties, which is itself a reason for His followers to praise Him. Focusing our vision and our worship beyond our trials to the One who dwells outside them provides a glimpse of another life — one that is not subject to sorrows or pain, one promised to all followers of Christ. Therefore, when God's people struggle with sin and its effects, we should turn our eyes toward the Lord above the heavens. Temptation beckons us to get caught up in sin's momentary pleasures and the pain of its results, but David's psalm calls us to fix our eyes on the exalted Lord who alone can provide a way through.

Psalm 109

When he is judged, let him come forth guilty,
And let his prayer become sin. — *Psalm 109:7*

In Psalm 109, David's rage is hard to ignore. The man after God's own heart asked God to take his enemy's life, make the man's children beggars, and even let the man's prayer "become sin" (Psalm 109:6–10)! How should we interpret and apply such biting pronouncements? First, we should remember that vengeance belongs to the Lord (Deuteronomy 32:35; Psalm 94:1). That David *prayed* his vengeful thoughts shows that he affirmed God's responsibility in this situation. Second, as Christians, we should remember our belief that God poured out on Jesus His vengeance and judgment for the sin of humanity. Our belief in the saving power of Jesus's crucifixion is a profound recognition of our own sin against God. In this light, psalms such as 109 become more about the struggle with ourselves than our enemies. Such psalms remind us in vivid detail of both the judgment we deserve and the compassion God provides.

Psalm 110

The Lord will stretch forth Your strong scepter from Zion, saying,
"Rule in the midst of Your enemies."   —*Psalm 110:2*

Kings rule. But, do they? In our world where kings have increasingly less power, it's difficult to wrap our minds around all it means to live under a king's authority. In Psalm 110, David invokes the image of a scepter to establish the authority of the ruling Davidic king, who was to stand amidst his enemies and rule with the approval of God behind him. In times past, this ideal failed as kings chose to follow their own paths. However, the ultimate Davidic king will one day perfectly embody this royal portrait. At that time, we too will live under this Davidic king—Jesus Himself. Our anticipation of His future rule should produce obedience—a difficult prospect, since we aren't in the habit of obeying earthly rulers and have wills that prefer to go their own directions. Therefore, to thrive as believers, we must get in the habit of submitting our wills to His and living as followers of Jesus rather than leaders of our own lives.

Psalm 111

Praise the LORD!
I will give thanks to the LORD with all my heart,
In the company of the upright and in the assembly. —Psalm 111:1

The psalmist called the people to praise God and give Him thanks in the presence of "the upright." The Hebrew term translated "upright" carries the sense of following a straight path. In other words, the psalmist expected God's people—those who praised and thanked God—to also be a people who followed the Lord along the narrow path. Praise, thanksgiving, and uprightness should never be separated. As we think about our identity before God, we recognize that He has made us a people called out to a new kind of life. We should keep ourselves on a narrow path, not just in what we believe but in how we choose to live. Further, we need to think about this, not just as individuals but also in terms of our collective identity as the church. How can we help Christian communities better live out the uprightness God expects of His people?

Psalm 112

It is well with the man who is gracious and lends;
He will maintain his cause in judgment. —Psalm 112:5

When the topic of generosity comes up, we immediately think of our possessions. And certainly, we can give of our own coffers. But being a giving person involves much more than just the transfer of goods. We can also generously give the intangible, including our good opinion. How often do we withhold the benefit of the doubt, showing ourselves as ungracious as the person or group we're vilifying? In the end, we're the ones angry, frustrated, and annoyed. Part of the value in being a generous person involves the personal benefit that comes from giving: wellness. As the psalmist says, "It is well with the man who is gracious and lends" (Psalm 112:5). When we live according to a code of graciousness—practicing generosity with our judgment and our possessions—we ensure that we will be in a good place as human beings . . . for good human beings embody grace.

Psalm 113

Who humbles Himself to behold
The things that are in heaven and in the earth? —*Psalm 113:6*

God sits enthroned in heaven, high above the small concerns of humanity. But our God is not one to forget His creation. He cares for our well-being, and while our struggles might be small compared to Him, He still considers them important. How do we know? The Lord humbles Himself—stoops down—to behold and interact with His creation, most significantly in the person of Jesus. To emulate God's concern for His creation, we too must look beyond ourselves to the needs and realities of others. However, our inclination is to hold ourselves above all others, viewing ourselves as lords of our domains and rarely looking beyond our own worlds. To humble ourselves, therefore, we must intentionally look to our God, who was not too grand to humble Himself, and ask for help in becoming more like Him. If He in all His greatness stoops down, we in our paltry splendor can surely follow His lead.

Psalm 114

Tremble, O earth, before the Lord,
Before the God of Jacob. —Psalm 114:7

When God led His people out of slavery in Egypt, nothing could stand in their way. Waters fled and armies recoiled while the mountains posed no obstacles. Everything and everyone submitted to God's plan for His people. The psalmist articulated the result of this movement into the Promised Land: the whole earth trembled before the Lord. One of the primary truths to come out of Israel's rescue from Egypt was that nothing can stand before the power of the Lord. All creation is under His authority and power. When we grapple with the reality that God's deeds lead the creation to tremble, it should change the way we approach our lives. Arrogance and self-determination bleed away in the face of the Creator's power. We recognize how small we truly are in the grand scheme of life and understand that worship and obedience are the only responses to this God, so great and mighty.

Psalm 115

But our God is in the heavens;
He does whatever He pleases. —Psalm 115:3

God's freedom rests at the heart of His character and His deeds. Our Lord is in heaven and He does whatever He pleases. This fact distinguishes God from the multiplicity of idols that have tempted people throughout the centuries. Where idols remain under the control of their makers, the true God keeps His own counsel, acting only in ways that He chooses. God delivers people from sin and shame because He wants to save them. God remains true to His word because He wants His word to be reliable. This reality frees us from the bonds of thinking that we can try to push God into action. While God graciously uses our requests to carry out His plan, He is not subject to our whims. This divine quality of freedom should prompt us to trust His sovereign plan rather than seek to manipulate it.

Psalm 116

What shall I render to the LORD
For all His benefits toward me? —Psalm 116:12

Gratitude stands as one of the most important responses we can make to our God. The psalmist related his deliverance from death, the greatest of threats, to bountiful or abundant life (Psalm 116:7–9). His response to God's good work in his life was to ask what he could do in return. The unmistakable gratitude expressed in his question sets boundaries for how we should live. When we have attitudes marked by gratitude, we invariably focus our attentions outward, rather than inward. The psalmist told of offering a sacrifice to keep the vow he made when the Lord rescued him in the midst of distress (116:17–18). Christians today aren't expected to offer sacrifices in the same way the Old Testament Israelites did. However, we are called to offer our lives as living sacrifices—something that becomes easier when we operate out of gratefulness for what God has done.

Psalm 117

Praise the LORD, all nations;
Laud Him, all peoples! —Psalm 117:1

God has always intended for all of humanity to worship Him. Although Abraham's descendants were chosen and set apart during the Old Testament era, the plan was always for Israel to stand as a beacon and a call to *all* nations. And the plan made great sense! Israel's central location on the eastern shore of the Mediterranean Sea allowed it easy access to people of a wide variety of nationalities, particularly travelers between Africa and Europe or Asia. Knowing that God's desire to redeem all of humanity has always been so, Christians today stand in unison with God's people in the Old Testament who proclaimed God's Word in both speech and deeds. Like Israel, we're to be beacons, and we take the gospel with us wherever we go, recognizing that God's message of salvation through Jesus is for everyone. May our faith in God as Deliverer increase our passion for people in our own nations and all over the world.

Psalm 118

The stone which the builders rejected
Has become the chief corner stone. — *Psalm 118:22*

It was true in ancient times, it was true for our Lord Jesus, and it remains true today: the path of righteousness leads to rejection. In Psalm 118, the psalmist used the image of a stone to picture the rejection of a suffering, righteous servant. The result of such dreadful circumstances? Elevation to a place of prime importance—to "corner stone." As communal beings, we fear rejection because rejection brings loneliness. This leads us, at times, to compromise righteousness in favor of acceptance. However, this psalm—and its connection to Jesus in 1 Peter 2:7—reminds us that while God's path leads to rejection by some, those who follow closely will retain His approval. We can trust that even if we are rejected by others, God remains at work in our lives.

Ultimately, however, this promise of rejection requires us each to answer a simple question: *At what cost will I follow Jesus?*

Psalm 119

I will never forget Your precepts,
For by them You have revived me.　　　　　*—Psalm 119:93*

The famously lengthy Psalm 119 spills much ink delighting in God's Word. Variously referred to as statutes, commandments, judgments, precepts, and more, the Word of God takes center stage in the psalm. And the psalm has much to teach us about God's Word—it guides (Psalm 119:105), it protects (119:11), and it strengthens (119:28). God's Word is also life-giving—we might even say resurrecting (119:93). Through His Word, the Lord brings life to His people, just as He brought life to earth through His word at creation (Genesis 1). As believers, we should cling to the life-giving power of God's Word. Not only do we personally struggle through periods of doubt and depression, but we are surrounded by people who have similar struggles. God's Word can speak light and hope into the darkness that often encroaches on our lives—it's just the kinds of words we need in our minds and hearts.

Psalm 120

Too long has my soul had its dwelling
With those who hate peace.
I am for peace, but when I speak,
They are for war.　　　　　*—Psalm 120:6–7*

In our day and age, we have become increasingly comfortable with images and expressions of warfare. We lace our words with warlike metaphors and act aggressively toward those who are different from us. Being an active force for peace gets passed over in favor of impulsive anger. As human beings, we must recognize that we are all different from one another, and that peace, therefore, means living with an attitude of love and kindness toward neighbors who act in contrast to our own ways. God calls us to be a people of peace, even if, like the psalmist, we are surrounded by warring parties. Actively seeking peace gives relationships with others precedence over the need to be right. Therefore, we must strive to live at peace with everyone, even if we disagree about significant spiritual or social issues (Romans 12:18; Hebrews 12:14).

Psalm 121

My help comes from the Lord,
Who made heaven and earth.
He will not allow your foot to slip;
He who keeps you will not slumber.   —*Psalm 121:2–3*

Our God never rests. He always remains active, working out His purposes and plans for His creation. As the people sang this "song of ascents" on their uphill journey from the Jordan River to worship at the temple in Jerusalem, the Lord's not allowing their feet to slip would have had special relevance (Psalm 121:3). But ancient people also struggled to stay on the narrow path of righteousness, just like we do today. For we who are prone to stumbling, the truth that our God is always working to keep us upright should give us comfort. More than that, it should spur us on to worship. God's constant activity on our behalf should create within us a desire to actively pursue Him and His desires for us. God does not slumber in keeping His people. Neither should we rest as we ascend from the depths of sin and death to the higher ground of purity and life.

Psalm 122

Our feet are standing
Within your gates, O Jerusalem,
Jerusalem, that is built
As a city that is compact together.　　　　　*—Psalm 122:2–3*

Psalm 122 would have been sung during one of the important feasts in Israel's calendar, when Jerusalem would have been stuffed with people. The city's high walls would have created a sense of closeness among the many worshipers. In fact, there would have been little room to move freely as worshipers pressed in alongside one another. The masses descending on the Holy City remind us that like the Israelites of old, we are a community of people who gather around a common object of worship. Today, God's people gather in smaller groups dotted across the globe. In cities and towns and speaking in varied languages, Christians offer praise and thanks to God. In each of these churches or "cities," we should seek to emulate that "compact" city of old Jerusalem—mirroring Old Testament worship by coming together in our churches and holding fast to the deep spiritual bond we share with our brothers and sisters in Christ.

Psalm 123

To You I lift up my eyes,
O You who are enthroned in the heavens!　　　　　*—Psalm 123:1*

The psalmist lifted his eyes, a natural movement when travelling uphill to Jerusalem, as he would have been when the people sang this "song of ascent." His mind was consumed with a vision of the sovereign ruling Lord. In the psalmist's view, he existed under this rule and was humbling himself by going to worship. Where do you fix your sight? We live in a world surrounded by things that attract our vision. When we seek out favor or good feelings from these objects of attraction, we soon realize that they cannot provide what their apparent beauty promises. In these moments, with our vision untethered from the Lord, we lose our spiritual footing and transfer our worship to something or someone other than God. With the lure of such fleeting beauty always around us, we must intentionally fix our sight on God as we seek His mercy and deliverance.

Psalm 124

"Had it not been the Lord who was on our side . . ." — Psalm 124:1

The Israelites recognized that the Lord was on their side. He wanted good for His people then, just as He desires good for His people today. Undoubtedly, God has always been on the side of His people. This has not prevented His judgment upon them for their sin, but even in judgment, He has never abandoned them. Even when the Israelites were enslaved in Egypt or exiled in Babylon, God remained with them, both times bringing them back into the Promised Land. With such evidence of God's faithfulness at hand, it would seem that we would easily place our confidence in Him. Yet, as circumstances turn against us, we sometimes wonder if He is out to get us. In the midst of those kinds of doubts, having the repeated, biblical reminder that the Lord truly is on our side can help us proceed with life confident in His faithfulness.

Psalm 125

*Those who trust in the L*ORD
Are as Mount Zion, which cannot be moved but abides forever.
—*Psalm 125:1*

During the mountain ascent to Jerusalem, Israelites bound for the temple sang this Psalm expressing their confidence in the Lord. The strong, immovable mountains that surrounded the travelers would have made for a powerful image of stability in the ancient world, just as they do today. The temple in Jerusalem rested upon Mount Zion, which means the psalmist was identifying Old Testament believers with the dwelling place of God. Today, when we trust in Jesus, He sends us the indwelling Holy Spirit—a truth that builds on this psalmic idea of God's people as God's dwelling place. We who follow Jesus as Savior and Lord carry God with us in fulfillment of Jesus's promise to the disciples (John 14:16). The Spirit helps us to trust God well, and that trust keeps us as stable as mountains. As we experience the ups and downs of life, we who believe can remember and know the Spirit's stabilizing presence within us.

Psalm 126

He who goes to and fro weeping, carrying his bag of seed,
Shall indeed come again with a shout of joy, bringing his sheaves
*   with him.* —*Psalm 126:6*

This song of celebration about God's restoration of His exiled people would have reminded the Israelites of a significant truth: God visits the suffering and ultimately delivers them unto joy. However, with deliverance comes continued responsibility. Notice that in Psalm 126, he who suffers carries seed into the fields and returns with sheaves. The abundance of the harvest serves as a potent image of joy for the newly-returned exiles. But to receive a return, the people had to first plant their seeds. The image of placing those seeds into the ground mirrors beautifully our struggle of placing our trust in the Lord—we have to give something valuable of our own with only the hope of receiving back something greater. As we await God's ultimate redemption of this fallen world, we must continue to sow the seeds of trust. If we do, we will reap a bountiful harvest of blessing in the life to come.

Psalm 127

Behold, children are a gift of the LORD,
The fruit of the womb is a reward.   *—Psalm 127:3*

Psalm 127 contrasts the anxieties of life (Psalm 127:1–2) with the blessings of life (127:3–5). Those who love life and give life to others will find themselves surrounded by gifts—their children. While many today do desire and yearn for children, it has become increasingly common for couples—even Christian couples—to choose to remain childless. Such a choice, when made despite good health and reproductive ability, is akin to choosing to become a fruit tree that bears no fruit. It denies the nature that God gave us at creation—not to mention His command to humanity to be fruitful and multiply (Genesis 1:28). Our commitment to children in the context of marriage mirrors our confession of new life in Jesus. When physically capable couples affirm life by giving it, they also affirm their commitment to others outside of themselves—a commitment that stands at the very heart of our Christian faith (Matthew 22:39).

116

Psalm 128

When you shall eat of the fruit of your hands,
You will be happy and it will be well with you.   *—Psalm 128:2*

God's blessings come to us in a variety of ways. Children, security, and deliverance from troubles all serve as obvious blessings in our lives. On the other hand, we often see work as anything but blessing. Sin and laziness have skewed our vision of work, but although the Lord cursed us by making work difficult as a result of the fall (Genesis 3:17–19), work itself was always part of God's perfect design—even before sin entered the world (2:15). Hard work, while difficult, produces great satisfaction in our ability to provide for ourselves and for those who depend upon us. As we think about our work—both in the home and outside it—we should think of it in the context of provision. We should take pride in and be grateful for our work for its ability to put food in our bellies, clothes on our backs, and roofs over our heads. Our work matters because we serve eternal humanity.

Psalm 129

May all who hate Zion
Be put to shame and turned backward.   *—Psalm 129:5*

When it comes to following Christ, does the community around us matter? Does a compromised community have an impact on our ability or inclination to follow God faithfully? The psalmist answered both of these questions with a resounding *yes*. Surrounded by people who tried to diminish him and his people, the psalmist asked that those who hated Zion—those who hated the plans and ideals of God—be "turned backward," or, in other words, removed from the community. The proper place for those who despise God's plan is outside the community of His people. Some will infiltrate our ranks with shallow, cultural Christianity, while others will openly challenge our convictions. As we look at our church communities, we need to ask whether they are places of purity—not places of perfection, but places where God's people are honestly and faithfully following Jesus.

Psalm 130

If You, LORD, should mark iniquities,
O Lord, who could stand?   *—Psalm 130:3*

When worshipers approach the one true and holy God to offer praise and thanks, we must come to Him in truth. One of the great failures of modern-day, western society is its embrace of the goodness of humanity while ignoring the wickedness that dwells in all of us. Psalm 130 reminds us that no one is righteous. All human beings have chosen outsider status with God. The worshipers singing Psalm 130 on the way to a temple festival in Jerusalem recognized their own sinfulness. And yet, in that recognition of sin, they also remembered that God makes Himself known to humans through His forgiveness (Psalm 130:4). These worshipers dared to approach their holy God only because they knew Him as a forgiving God. When we recognize ourselves for who we actually are—sinners in need of forgiveness—we can more clearly see God for who He actually is—a deity who loves to forgive.

Psalm 131

O Lord, my heart is not proud, nor my eyes haughty;
Nor do I involve myself in great matters,
Or in things too difficult for me. —Psalm 131:1

David understood pride through the hard experience of failure. His pride led him to sin against God, and it came naturally to the king. Over time, he had to learn the habit of humility. In our pride, we strive for understanding, material things, and power well beyond our reach. Pride prompts us to promote ourselves over God. This psalm reminds us that we must approach life in the proper spirit—one of humility rather than pride, stillness rather than striving (Psalm 131:2). Such an approach presumes a deep contentment within us that overcomes all our anxieties about all that remains mysterious around us. When we trust in ourselves rather than God, however, we struggle to content our hearts, always believing there is one more thing we can do to take control of our circumstances. While we continue to strive for knowledge, understanding, jobs, and achievements, we must always recognize God's continued sovereignty over our lives.

Psalm 132

The Lord has sworn to David
A truth from which He will not turn back:
"Of the fruit of your body I will set upon your throne."
—Psalm 132:11

David's great—and ultimately, unfulfilled—desire was to build a dwelling place for God in Jerusalem (Psalm 132:5). David's concern for the establishment of that house of worship mirrors

God's concern for establishing David's lineage on the throne of Israel. King David first illustrated his desire to build the temple by bringing the tabernacle — God's temporary dwelling place — into the Holy City (2 Samuel 6:12–15). Later, after God revealed He wouldn't allow David to build the temple, the king still gathered all the materials for its construction (1 Chronicles 22:5). Although David didn't see his dream fulfilled, God kept His word by allowing the king's sons to rule. And the ultimate result of David's sacrificial perspective is bound up in his descendent Jesus Christ, who will sit on the throne forever (Psalm 132:12). Therefore, as we confess Jesus as Lord, we affirm our confidence that God will keep His word, and we allow into our lives one more outlet of hope.

Psalm 133

Behold, how good and how pleasant it is
For brothers to dwell together in unity!　　　　　—Psalm 133:1

Another of the "songs of ascent," Psalm 133 embraces the unity of God's people as they traveled to Jerusalem for worship. Israelites from all over the nation would have made the journey, giving the celebration of unity even greater significance. Because families from different tribes would have traveled to Jerusalem shoulder to shoulder, good relations were essential during this time devoted to the special worship. But even as these tribal members walked together, their distinctions were never erased—each represented their own tribe, even as they represented Israel as a whole. This psalm reminds us that God values unity, but He does not demand uniformity. Differences between people today—political, cultural, and racial—sometimes tempt us into desiring uniformity. But the distinctions between Christians, who all believe in and follow Jesus, offer opportunities for understanding, compassion, and patience that uniformity simply wouldn't allow.

Psalm 134

Behold, bless the LORD, all servants of the LORD,
Who serve by night in the house of the LORD! —*Psalm 134:1*

This conclusion to the section of "songs of ascent" encourages priests to lead the people in worship. The psalmist encouraged these leaders to worship even in the black of night—revealing an expectation that we should see all hours of the day as opportunities to worship. God still dwells in heaven during the night, just as He does in the day. We should not relegate worship and living in light of God's ways, therefore, to particular times of the day or week. God doesn't just want His people to worship on Sunday mornings or even just during the hours between sunrise and sunset. As a way of dedicating our lives to God, worship should take place at any and every time for us who profess faith in the Lord. When we look to our leaders in the church, we should perceive that same level of commitment—a complete devotion to following Jesus.

Psalm 135

Those who make them will be like them,
Yes, everyone who trusts in them. —*Psalm 135:18*

On the heels of a section describing God's acts in the world (Psalm 135:5–14), the psalmist included a contrasting section on the inaction of idols. God has done great works of creation and redemption, but idols are blind, deaf, dumb, and dead.

The real tragedy of idols, however, is not their inability to do anything, but rather the way they influence God's most magnificent creation — humanity. We take on the characteristics of that which we worship. So if we worship something besides God, instead of enjoying full and rich lives engaged in the world and using our capabilities to the fullest, we become blind, deaf, dumb, and dead. We become just like our idols themselves. While believers today do not always have carved images to contend with, we still set any number of things above God, and the result is the same . . . death in place of life.

Psalm 136

Give thanks to the God of heaven,
For His lovingkindness is everlasting.   —*Psalm 136:26*

We sometimes focus too much on God in the abstract. We think of His invisible attributes, His nature, His essence. But while these are useful subjects to ponder, we run into problems when we forget about the concrete ways God has made Himself known in the world. The psalmist listed several of these tangible evidences of God's loving-kindness — the creation of the earth, the deliverance of Israel from Egypt, and the securing of the Promised Land. These historical events root our understanding of God in the physical world around us rather than simply in the world of ideas in our minds. God the Father is a real person, who has truly acted in our world throughout history — just as He acts in our hearts by the Holy Spirit today. Let's take a cue from the psalmist and relate to God through these this-world events. Therein we may find a much closer connection with the Creator.

Psalm 137

*How can we sing the L*ORD*'s song*
In a foreign land? —*Psalm 137:4*

When the people of Judah were exiled to Babylon in 586 BC, they lost more than their access to the Promised Land. They also lost their joy. Under the torments of their captors, God's people mourned the lack of God's blessing in their lives. They wondered how they could sing songs of praise for the land God had given them—the memory of that place was just too painful for a people in a foreign land and under God's judgment (Psalm 137:4). The question remains a potent one today. The Bible refers to people of faith as strangers in search of a better, heavenly country (Hebrews 11:13–16). We, like those exiles of old, sometimes mourn what could have been had our sin not tainted God's creation. We must remember, however, that our hope is in God and in the redeemed world to come—a truth that remains vibrant even when the songs stick in our throats.

Psalm 138

*For though the L*ORD *is exalted,*
Yet He regards the lowly,
But the haughty He knows from afar. —*Psalm 138:6*

In Psalm 138, David acknowledged God's high position over all creation. That alone was reason enough to make the Lord worthy of praise. However, God does not remain removed from all people, as David observed. God regards, or sees, the lowly and the humble (Psalm 138:6). Humility can refer to a chosen attitude, but it can also refer to those who have fallen into humble—or humbling—circumstances. For this group,

David made clear that God had not lost sight of them. On the other hand, God distances Himself from the haughty—those of more exalted circumstances who believe they can take care of themselves. When we fall on hard times, David's words comfort us—God is with us, no matter how far we fall. These words should also encourage within us an attitude of humility and dependence in contrast to the pride of those who depend only upon themselves.

Psalm 139

Do I not hate those who hate You, O LORD?
And do I not loathe those who rise up against You?
I hate them with the utmost hatred;
They have become my enemies.　　　　　　*—Psalm 139:21–22*

David expressed an honest desire for God to act against his enemies. In the Bible, *hatred* most often indicates rejection. So David, believing himself on God's side, prayed for the Lord to act in a way that would affirm the king's position. In short, David wanted to reject those that God rejected. We have no access to the results of David's prayer—no knowledge whether or not God acted on His servant's behalf. Instead, we have David's cry for God to search him and direct his thoughts. David was open to correction, but the possibility about being wrong didn't stop him from praying what was in his heart. We sometimes tiptoe around God, afraid to share with Him our deepest desires. But humility doesn't require that we walk on eggshells. David's strongly worded prayer encourages us to express our thoughts to God, while always doing our best to stay in accord with His will.

Psalm 140

I said to the Lord, "You are my God;
Give ear, O Lord, to the voice of my supplications." — *Psalm 140:6*

Caught in the traps and schemes of evil men, David knew where to turn, and he trusted the Lord would hear his prayers. David approached God with the confidence of one who understood God's way of doing things. When David asked God to listen to his supplications, he was asking the Lord to grant him favor. In other words, David saw himself as inferior to God's superior wisdom and ability to deal with life's problems. David immediately followed his confidence in God's hearing this prayer with confidence that the Lord had already prepared him for battle (Psalm 140:7). While none of us wish for difficult circumstances to come into our lives, we know that trials and temptations will certainly find us. And when life turns south and God seems silent, we can have faith that the Lord will indeed give ear to all our supplications and care for us as we approach Him with humility and confidence.

Psalm 141

Set a guard, O Lord, over my mouth;
Keep watch over the door of my lips. — *Psalm 141:3*

On the heels of requesting that God listen to his prayer, David asked God to guard his mouth and keep watch over the door of his lips. David recognized the double-edged sword of the human mouth. In one moment, we can offer heartfelt prayers that exhibit great trust in God's deliverance and power, and in the next, we can offer stinging words that tear down God's image-bearers and bring shame to a God who deserves only honor. David pictured his mouth as a powerful instrument that required someone to guard it and watch for what might come out. The ease with which we can open our mouths and expel damaging barbs should prompt us to pray David's prayer too. All of us could make better use of this powerful, God-given instrument. How would our families, churches, and communities change if we earnestly desired for the Lord to stand watch over our tongues?

Psalm 142

"Bring my soul out of prison,
So that I may give thanks to Your name;
The righteous will surround me,
For You will deal bountifully with me."   —*Psalm 142:7*

David wrote this psalm while reflecting on his time spent cave-bound while on the run from Saul (1 Samuel 22:1; 24:3). With the enemies of God waiting for David to show himself in the light, the future king reflected on his imprisonment in the darkness. He hoped for a time when he might give thanks to the Lord in the light. But deliverance for David meant more than simply leaving the cave. It also meant being surrounded by the righteous. David looked forward to a time when God's people would come alongside him in support and love. As we think about our own deliverance from the bondage of sin, we too look for the righteous to surround us through God's church. And while no Christian experiences this in its fullness in this life—because sin remains prevalent, even among believers—we come together in the church, hoping for a community of righteousness and striving to embody just that.

Psalm 143

Teach me to do Your will,
For You are my God;
Let Your good Spirit lead me on level ground. —*Psalm 143:10*

Many search high and low for God's will, but the reality is that God's desires for our lives aren't hard to sniff out. Lists like the fruit of the Spirit and Jesus's commands in the Sermon on the Mount give us a clear idea of the kind of people the Lord expects us to be. Our problem, then, is not in knowing God's will but in learning to practice it day in and day out. David understood the ways that our personal desires often conflict with the righteous path God makes clear to us. So David asked God to help him embrace righteousness, not just in his words but also in his deeds. David's request for the Spirit's guidance mirrors Jesus's promise that after His ascension, the Spirit would come and serve as a guide for us (John 16:7–11). Let us each embody righteousness by relying on the Spirit's ministry of guidance.

Psalm 144

Let our sons in their youth be as grown-up plants,
And our daughters as corner pillars fashioned as for a palace.
—*Psalm 144:12*

All parents have goals for their children. Some goals are worthy for any child; others are motivated by personal preference. David's Psalm 144 provides two beautifully stated goals. He asked for his sons to be as "grown-up plants" and for his daughters to be as "corner pillars fashioned as for a palace" (Psalm 144:12). The picture of plants evokes ideas of health, strength, and fruitfulness. The image of pillars suggests stateliness, beauty, and stability. If you're a parent, what do you pray for your children? The goals we hold for our children should correspond with David's. Parents should use this verse and others like it as starting points in their prayers for their children. And we should all search the Scriptures for what they say about the character of good children and set out to help the children in our lives embody that character in their own lives.

Psalm 145

The LORD is good to all,
And His mercies are over all His works.   *—Psalm 145:9*

That each of us exists at all is a mercy of God. When we think about the many ways in which we have failed God, our vision sharpens and we can see His mercies in our lives all the more clearly. However, His mercy is on *every* life and *every* created thing. David testified to God's mercy upon all His works (Psalm 145:9). If that is actually true—and it is, given that this declaration in Scripture ultimately came from God—then part of our job is to see God's mercy in the existence of everything in His creation. Easier said than done, especially when we witness decay in the created world, experience struggle in our relationships, and perceive the depths of our own faults. Training our eyes to see God's mercy on all should change our vision of how we relate to others . . . and to our world.

Psalm 146

The Lord protects the strangers;
He supports the fatherless and the widow,
But He thwarts the way of the wicked.   —*Psalm 146:9*

God cares for the very people many of us ignore or avoid, and because He sustains those in need, the Lord will always be worthy of praise. We all know the uncomfortable feeling of being a stranger in a new place. A smaller group of us understand the displacing feelings that come with losing a parent as a child . . . or losing a spouse . . . or finding ourselves completely alone and vulnerable. God makes His presence known to those who are absolutely defenseless in the world, as Old Testament widows and orphans were. The wicked, on the other hand, find in God an obstacle to their dark pursuits. For those of us who know too well a category like the ones the psalmist mentioned, the application is clear: God cares for the needy, and He thwarts the wicked. As for the rest of us, we need to care for those in need and become an obstacle to wickedness.

Psalm 147

He does not delight in the strength of the horse;
He does not take pleasure in the legs of a man.   —*Psalm 147:10*

We can all appreciate the beauty and intelligence that went into the creation of horses and humans. We find good in both, and it makes sense—God made them, so how could we not? However, God's delight in His creation doesn't stem from its great feats of strength or impressive displays of endurance. Instead, God pours out His favor upon those who respect Him and look to Him for grace (Psalm 147:11). Therefore, God's "negative" view of horses and humans in this psalm isn't actually negative at all. Rather, the psalmist used this language to offer a critique of those who depend on their own strength, something God doesn't look upon with kindness. As we follow the Lord in our day-to-day lives, one of the most difficult tasks we face is depending on His strength rather than our own. The psalmist's words should encourage us to foster that attitude of dependence.

Psalm 148

Let them praise the name of the LORD,
For His name alone is exalted;
His glory is above earth and heaven.   —*Psalm 148:13*

God is worthy of praise because He gave life and existence to every element of our world. The psalmist detailed aspects of creation, from the stars in the highest heavens to the "old men and children" who walk the earth (Psalm 148:12). For every one of these created things, the expectation is the same: praise the Lord. Everything that God has made was created to give Him praise by completely being what He made them to be. A star gives God praise by completely embodying its star-ness. A tree gives God praise by being everything that tree was intended to be. And while these things praise God naturally and without the struggle that humans have, we can learn from the rest of creation. Just as other created animals and things embody all that God made them to be, so too should we praise God by embodying all that He made us to be—people of faith, hope, and especially love.

Psalm 149

To execute on them the judgment written;
This is an honor for all His godly ones.
Praise the LORD! — Psalm 149:9

We tend to think of God's judgment as an unpleasant future reality that we will have to endure. However, the psalmist spoke of God's judgment in the context of praise. Using vivid imagery of two-edged swords for battle and fetters for government officials, the psalmist praised the Lord in advance for the opportunity to judge those who set themselves against the Almighty (Psalm 149:6–8). The privilege of joining God in His righteous judgment of the world comes only to the godly. As we follow God, we do so out of love for Him and a desire to please Him. But we also look forward to being on the right side of the coming judgment, knowing that while God has been merciful in allowing people the opportunity to respond to His call to salvation, He will eventually bring this era to a close with judgment on those who have persisted in their wicked ways.

Psalm 150

Praise Him with loud cymbals;
Praise Him with resounding cymbals.
Let everything that has breath praise the LORD.
Praise the LORD! — Psalm 150:5–6

The psalmist listed instrument after instrument in this exhortation to bring praise to the God over all. The psalm gives the overwhelming sense that the people should be so filled with desire to praise the Lord that they will pick up *anything* around them in order to make a joyful noise in His honor. And praise not only happens with a variety of instruments, literal and makeshift, in the sanctuary of worship. The psalmist encouraged his readers to remember that praise for God happens *anywhere*—even in the heavens themselves (Psalm 150:1). Human beings have a long history of music-making, and music is one of the great gifts that God has given us. Therefore, let us use music to praise the Lord! And may we make that music an extension of us, throwing not just our voices but all our physical strength and skill into the praise of the Almighty.

Proverbs

Proverbs 1

The fear of the LORD is the beginning of knowledge;
Fools despise wisdom and instruction.   — *Proverbs 1:7*

The Proverbs are collections of wise sayings that stand unique in the Bible's Wisdom Books. Short, pithy, practical, and powerful, proverbs are not promises to claim but principles to apply. They remain generally true in every generation and yet allow for life's exceptions, often without explanation or apology. The book of Proverbs opens by proclaiming its purpose to bestow wisdom on the reader who applies diligence in seeking it (Proverbs 1:1–6). "The fear of the LORD is the beginning of knowledge" (1:7) remains a maxim as true today as it was when Solomon wrote it. The saying refers not to a beginning from which one departs but to a foundation upon which all knowledge must build—and to the standard by which all decisions should be made. "Fear" here indicates not terror but rather respect and awe—the appropriate state for one in relationship to God.

Proverbs 2

The LORD gives wisdom;
From His mouth come knowledge and understanding.
He stores up sound wisdom for the upright;
He is a shield to those who walk in integrity.   — *Proverbs 2:6–7*

The source of wisdom springs from revelation. Only God offers knowledge and understanding, and only the upright are prepared to receive it. Growing in wisdom occurs not from emptying one's mind but from filling it with revealed truth. Finding wisdom requires searching for it where God has marked the X—like searching for silver and hidden treasure (Proverbs 2:4). That kind of digging takes diligence and hard work. New Bible translations, books, and conferences may give the impression that they hold the secret to unlocking the wisdom of God's Word, but Proverbs reminds us there are no shortcuts to spirituality. We must personally spend time in the Bible to personally profit from it. The benefits of the search yield a wealth far more valuable than money. Wisdom's riches offer discernment that guides us into "every good course" (Proverbs 2:9) and that guards us from the long-term fallout of foolish, short-term pleasures (2:11–18).

Proverbs 3

*Trust in the L*ORD *with all your heart*
And do not lean on your own understanding.
In all your ways acknowledge Him,
And He will make your paths straight.
Do not be wise in your own eyes;
*Fear the L*ORD *and turn away from evil.*   *—Proverbs 3:5–7*

Perhaps the book's most famous verses, these words carry with them one of the toughest assignments. Trusting the Lord, in context, refers to trusting what He has revealed. Our temptation lies in trusting—or believing—we know better. These three verses volley between positive and negative commands, balancing wisdom in between the parallel thoughts. Positively, we are to trust in the Lord and acknowledge Him—with all our hearts and in all our ways. The repeated "all" excludes exceptions, an important detail to note when life hurls situations at us that seem to defy God's Word. In those moments, we must refuse to lean on our own understanding or to be wise in our own eyes, trusting that God has our best interests in mind and He will direct our paths. Wisdom's foundation rests on fearing the Lord and turning away from evil, two sides of the same coin—one never present without the other.

Proverbs 4

Hear, my son, and accept my sayings
And the years of your life will be many. . . .
My son, give attention to my words;
Incline your ear to my sayings.   *—Proverbs 4:10, 20*

"My son . . . my son," repeated the writer. Twenty-three times the phrase "my son" appears in the book of Proverbs, driving home the truth that while wisdom's source ultimately comes from God, children's first exposure to wisdom comes from their parents. Godly parents understand their responsibility to do more than live good lives and convey eternal truths (Deuteronomy 6:7; Ephesians 6:4). Godly parenting requires intentionality and love. It occurs not only in heated moments of correction but also (and best) in moments of emotional warmth. The conversation of Proverbs 4 displays a tone of honesty, concern, consistency, and kindness—all essential to effective parental influence. Like the father in Proverbs, we must practice a warm love as we warn our children to guard their hearts (Proverbs 4:23), because their hearts control what they say (4:24), what they see (4:25), and where they go (4:26–27).

Proverbs 5

Drink water from your own cistern
And fresh water from your own well. . . .
Let your fountain be blessed,
And rejoice in the wife of your youth.   *—Proverbs 5:15, 18*

The godly father in Proverbs excluded no warning from his son. In chapter 5, the father likened thirst for water to sensual desire.

Drawing metaphorically from a cistern, a well, and a spring, he told his son that the source from which a man drinks to satisfy desire will bring either life or death. The illustration exposes adultery as both wasteful—"Should your springs overflow in the streets?" (Proverbs 5:16 NIV)—and needless, for God gives a husband all he needs in his marriage. Further, God commands the man to "be exhilarated" with his wife, or literally "intoxicated," which intensifies the drinking metaphor (5:19). Some truths never change. Our acts of passion reveal our spiritual well-being, and choosing the wrong outlet for our passion ushers in permanent consequences. Sensuality longs for both a physical *and* lasting satisfaction—a compelling reason why we needn't look beyond our spouses to slake the thirst God created marriage to satisfy.

Proverbs 6

"A little sleep, a little slumber,
A little folding of the hands to rest"—
Your poverty will come in like a vagabond
And your need like an armed man.   *—Proverbs 6:10–11*

The repeated word *little* reveals the sluggard's flawed justification for slacking off. After all, it's only a little! But this passage warns us that wisdom guards against such rationalizations for sidestepping responsibility. Most of life's regrets come from slow leaks, not blowouts. Just as the results of hard work aren't immediate, neither are the results of laziness. Both diligence and laziness bring results. Little things add up either way. And like the straw that broke the proverbial camel's back, a negligent lifestyle eventually brings an unexpected collapse. The outcome shouldn't take us by surprise, but it does, leaving us feeling like we've been robbed by "an armed man." May we instead be like the ant that "prepares" and "gathers" its food little by little (Proverbs 6:6 – 8). The discipline of consistency adds up, and it will be a blessing in a season of need (13:11).

Proverbs 7

Do not let your heart turn aside to her ways,
Do not stray into her paths.
For many are the victims she has cast down,
And numerous are all her slain.   —*Proverbs 7:25 – 26*

The father exhorted his naïve son to imagine himself in the place of tragedy. After all, it could happen to any man (or woman) who fails to follow the principles in these verses. First, the father urged his son to refuse to allow his heart to "turn aside to her ways." Adultery begins in a curious mind that dwells upon and longs for anything outside of God's will. Second, the son should keep himself physically away from temptation—"do not stray into her paths"—in order to curb any weakening of the moral resolve. Third, he should think beyond temptation's pleasure to the result of sin—death. One of Proverbs' repeated themes lies in wisdom's challenge to us to stand on tiptoe and look beyond the immediate to the long view, to the end of the path we're considering. Find the desired outcome, trace the path backward, and take it.

Proverbs 8

"Blessed is the man who listens to me,
Watching daily at my gates,
Waiting at my doorposts.
For he who finds me finds life
And obtains favor from the Lord*."*   *—Proverbs 8:34–35*

The eighth chapter of Proverbs opens with wisdom personified as a woman challenging naïve men to choose her way. In contrast to the ungodly woman who led the naïve to death in chapter 7, wisdom offers a way to life. God's creation of life came about through His wisdom (Proverbs 8:22–31), and living life as He intended it requires seeking the wisdom of God. In this proverb, wisdom calls out from convenient places where passersby cannot help but hear (8:1–3). Today, God's wisdom is distilled in the Scriptures—and in Jesus Christ (1 Corinthians 1:30). And the convenient access we have to God's Word—in study Bibles, Web sites, radio programs, and devotional books—offers wisdom for the taking. But acquiring wisdom requires more than buying a book or any other resource. To enjoy the benefits of wisdom, we must earnestly seek wisdom "daily"—literally, "day by day"—in the place we know it can be found: God's Word.

Proverbs 9

The fear of the Lord *is the beginning of wisdom,*
And the knowledge of the Holy One is understanding.
                                        —Proverbs 9:10

Chapter 9 offers a summary of the previous eight: only two paths exist in life—wisdom or folly. Wisdom calls to the naïve, inviting them to feast from her table, receive her reproofs, and grow in wisdom by considering the outcome of a life well lived (Proverbs 9:1–12). Folly also calls to the naïve, inviting them to feast at her table and presenting the half-truth that "stolen water is sweet" without warning of the consequences (9:17–18). Wedged between the presentation of these two choices in chapter 9, the book's maxim surfaces again: "The fear of the LORD is the beginning of wisdom" (9:10). Here, in contrast to 1:7, the word *beginning* reflects a starting point from which a wise person grows "still wiser" and "will increase his learning" (9:9). A relationship with God is the place to begin when choosing the path to walk and the place to continue looking to along the way.

Proverbs 10

A wise son makes a father glad,
But a foolish son is a grief to his mother.   —*Proverbs 10:1*

Godly parents model and teach the truth — as the "my son" lessons of Proverbs' early chapters reveal — but the acceptance or rejection of wisdom lies squarely with the child. Proverbs 10:1 reveals the lingering results of that acceptance or rejection on the parents. The antithetical phrasing of verse 1 shows that children's personal decisions affect people other than themselves. They spill over into the emotions of their parents. The same holds true for those younger in the faith whom older believers consider their "children" (3 John 4). The application is timeless: as children, our wise or foolish choices produce gladness or grief respectively in our parents — even after we leave home and begin our own families. Likewise, our children's choices impact us as adults. At every age, our daily decisions to follow wisdom or folly carry emotional triggers that travel back to our parental roots.

Proverbs 11

As a ring of gold in a swine's snout
So is a beautiful woman who lacks discretion.   —*Proverbs 11:22*

A woman's beauty should be used for God's glory. Esther modeled this well. Her looks afforded her a prestigious position that allowed her to persuade a godless king to save her people (Esther 2:2; 4:14). Proverbs 11 speaks to this same principle. The outrageous comparison in verse 22 links two creatures we would never compare. Swine represented disgusting, unclean animals to a Hebrew. The "ring of gold" was a nose ring, a common ornament for a Hebrew woman. Such a ring in the snout of a pig seems altogether inappropriate and comical—and it is. Today, we still admire gold rings and beautiful women, but this proverb forces us to look below the skin—at what God admires—to the heart. A modest woman shines more brightly than any adornment (1 Timothy 2:9–10; 1 Peter 3:3–4). And, just as a pig would quickly sully the luster of a gold ring, so indiscretion adds ugliness to those with only outward beauty.

Proverbs 12

He who tills his land will have plenty of bread,
But he who pursues worthless things lacks sense.   —*Proverbs 12:11*

Proverbs 12:11 explains the difference between the focused person and the distracted person. The focused farmer does one thing; he works his land. The result? He has plenty of bread. The other individual pursues "worthless things"—a phrase that's one word in Hebrew and means "empty." It's not that this person is lazy, because in Hebrew *pursues* is a rigorous verb. This is a busy man! But his interests are scattered, his time squandered, and the things he chases have no substance—they're empty. This proverb reveals the necessity of focus and, by principle, the need to eliminate the distractions that never-ending options give. Jesus modeled this well when He diminished His healing ministry to keep His preaching ministry a priority (Mark 1:38). Believers should follow suit, asking the Lord what He wants us to do and then giving that pursuit our full focus. We'll always have plenty of good deeds to do—so many that we could miss the purpose for which God has called us.

Proverbs 13

The soul of the sluggard craves and gets nothing,
But the soul of the diligent is made fat.　　　　*—Proverbs 13:4*

Everyone has ambitions and hopes. Even the sluggard "craves" for certain results in life, but because all he does is desire, he "gets nothing." The hard-working person, on the other hand, adds diligence to desire and gets the results. Along with persistence, diligence includes clarity of purpose and motivation for the goal. When obstacles challenge us to abandon our goals because the work seems too hard, wisdom reorients our commitment and renews our strength. The shortest path to success will always be the right path. There are no shortcuts to goals achieved or to dreams come true, and the wise individual will determine that accomplishing the goal is worth the hard work required. As this verse teaches, satisfaction comes only through diligence. And how does diligence begin? By simply determining every day to take the next step.

Proverbs 14

Where no oxen are, the manger is clean,
But much revenue comes by the strength of the ox. —*Proverbs 14:4*

Oxen are messy animals. They require care, feeding, shelter—and manure cleanup in spades. If a person focuses only on what the ox demands, it seems hard to justify keeping it. But the wisdom of perspective makes all the difference. Nobody likes shoveling dung, but everyone enjoys eating. The strength of the messy ox brings much revenue—a benefit that outweighs having to clean the manger. This principle reaches into most areas of life. Our closest relationships expose the messiest parts of our personalities, but without them our lives would be intensely lonely. Employees require a busy HR department, but our corporations would fail without them. Flawed leaders guide our government and churches, but without them, we would have lawlessness and no spiritual leaders. Before we contemplate selling the messy "ox," we should consider all he provides. Wisdom requires a willingness to sacrifice the joy of tidiness for the long-term benefits of productivity, provision, and growth.

Proverbs 15

Without consultation, plans are frustrated,
But with many counselors they succeed.   —*Proverbs 15:22*

This verse's theme appears four times in Proverbs, underscoring the significance of it in our lives (Proverbs 11:14; 20:18; 24:6). Making important plans without consulting trusted people for advice leads to frustration and, ultimately, failure. No one person understands all aspects of a situation, and plowing forward without consulting others—especially when the plans affect those people or require them for completion—is a setup for disappointment and disharmony. On the personal level, it's presumptuous and disrespectful. On the professional level, it smacks of self-sufficiency and communicates that we see others as insignificant. As Christians, success in the body of Christ requires each of us to utilize our spiritual gifts and to rely on the gifts of others (1 Corinthians 12:14–31). Wisdom utilizes the "many counselors" God provides, and it welcomes honest input rather than ear-tickling flattery and eager acquiescence (Proverbs 26:28; 27:6; 28:23; 29:5).

Proverbs 16

He who is slow to anger is better than the mighty,
And he who rules his spirit, than he who captures a city.
—*Proverbs 16:32*

In Solomon's day, "the mighty" and "he who captures a city" stood tall as national heroes. This level of military skill accomplished more than gaining admiration for those who possessed it. Such skill was essential to national security. The mighty men of Israel did incredible deeds when they defeated an enemy. In tandem with such an impressive illustration, this proverb measures the strength of one who can control his or her emotions as better than, or preferable to, the power of a military champion. Controlling one's temper is a virtue that goes beyond physical power to spiritual strength and godliness. In fact, the phrase "slow to anger" often describes the patience of God Himself (Exodus 34:6). The apostle James elaborated on this principle when he reminded us: "Everyone must be quick to hear, slow to speak and slow to anger; for the anger of man does not achieve the righteousness of God" (James 1:19–20).

Proverbs 17

The refining pot is for silver and the furnace for gold,
But the LORD tests hearts. —*Proverbs 17:3*

Just as fire reveals the dross of a precious metal so its impurities may be removed, so God tests our hearts so we may "extract the precious from the worthless" (Jeremiah 15:19). God tests our hearts through "fiery trials" (1 Peter 1:6–7; 4:12), and this ultimately brings about our good. The Divine Smelter purifies His people in many ways, sometimes by providing lack "that He might humble you, testing you, to know what was in your heart" (Deuteronomy 8:2) and sometimes through the praise of others (Proverbs 27:21). Proverbs 17:3 reveals a timeless truth for all believers: because God controls the fiery trials, we have the responsibility to respond to our revealed impurities with repentance (Jeremiah 26:29–30). At times, this process may feel cruel or "sorrowful; yet to those who have been trained by it, afterwards it yields the peaceful fruit of righteousness" (Hebrews 12:11).

Proverbs 18

A fool does not delight in understanding,
But only in revealing his own mind. . . .
He who gives an answer before he hears,
It is folly and shame to him. . . .
The first to plead his case seems right,
Until another comes and examines him. —*Proverbs 18:2, 13, 17*

Three times in chapter 18 we receive caution against forming hasty judgments. A foolish person speaks before understanding a situation, thus "revealing his own mind." The Hebrew verb used for "revealing" hints at indecency, as its only other use in Scripture occurs in the account of Noah's nakedness (Genesis 9:21). Speaking before listening reveals arrogance and eventually betrays ignorance. Self-important people assume too much about themselves, and then shame must teach by experience what wisdom attempted by instruction. Because truth is made up of parts, we must always remember to hear all sides of a situation before assuming we understand it. Even then, humility embraces the truth that only God knows all—including motives. As we face new situations, let's remember that human nature is selective, both in interpreting events and reporting them . . . and only fools assume to comprehend the whole puzzle when they've merely seen a single piece.

Proverbs 19

Cease listening, my son, to discipline,
And you will stray from the words of knowledge. —*Proverbs 19:27*

The Hebrew word rendered "stray" pictures a sheep that has wandered from the flock. Alone, helpless, vulnerable, and foolish, this creature has drifted from the shepherd's watch care. The term *discipline* refers to moral correction, an uncomfortable but essential requirement in every life. Proverbs 19:27 warns that failing to heed godly reproof will result in a person's straying from the path of wisdom to a road that Proverbs repeatedly warns as destructive. "Discipline" comes from God and remains an ongoing process in the life of each believer (Proverbs 3:11; Hebrews 12:5). Our Father disciplines us because we are His children and He loves us. The process is normal, necessary, and never-ending. At no point can we assume we no longer need discipline. Even Paul confessed he had not yet "arrived," while at the same time, he was mature (Philippians 3:12–16). The maturation process stops when we cease listening to discipline.

Proverbs 20

Man's steps are ordained by the L<small>ORD</small>,
How then can man understand his way? —*Proverbs 20:24*

God's sovereignty remains a source of confusion and comfort. It confuses us because we cannot comprehend how the blending of two wills—His and ours—effectively results in one. "How then can man understand his way?" We can't. But the doctrine of God's sovereignty also provides immense comfort. The steps we take, however prayerfully or foolishly chosen, will result in God's sovereign will for our lives. God promises that He ultimately affirms or overrides every choice we make (Proverbs 16:1, 9; 19:21). What's more, no evil done to us will ever thwart God's will for us, but rather, the evil we experience will somehow play a part in His plan to conform us to the image of His Son (Genesis 50:20; Romans 8:28–39; 11:33–36). Although we cannot understand *how* God's sovereignty works, we can understand *that* it does. Consequently, no matter what we face, we can respond with trust, obedience, and worship.

Proverbs 21

It is better to live in a corner of a roof
Than in a house shared with a contentious woman. . . .
It is better to live in a desert land
Than with a contentious and vexing woman. —*Proverbs 21:9, 19*

Marriage offers the highest joys and the deepest pains. These two proverbs compare two types of existence—humiliating solitude and insufferable company. Hebrew homes had second-story rooftops that served as open-air balconies. According to Proverbs 21, living exposed to the weather in a cramped corner of a roof surpasses the misery of sharing a house with a quarrelsome wife. And living in a desert — with all its lack — makes for a better existence than living with a vexing wife. The subject of a contentious wife also appears in chapter 19. The parallelism of the metaphors there suggests that a prickly wife is also a foolish one, for her nagging erodes her husband's well-being (Proverbs 19:13). The implication? God created us all for relationship and for peace. A woman sets the emotional atmosphere of the home ("If momma ain't happy . . ."), and her words, attitude, and actions make a difference for all who live there (14:1).

Proverbs 22

Incline your ear and hear the words of the wise,
And apply your mind to my knowledge;
For it will be pleasant if you keep them within you,
That they may be ready on your lips.
So that your trust may be in the LORD.   —*Proverbs 22:17–19*

While reading the Proverbs, we must remember that the danger we have to remain aware of actually occurs *after* we finish reading . . . when we think our job is done. Hearing the truth only begins the process. The commands to "hear" and "apply the mind" infer that our goal must go beyond information to transformation. After listening with attentive concentration, we must determine to remember the truth in principle — if not also by memorization. Such personal retention will allow us to speak truth in moments of need (Proverbs 22:18), maintain our trust in God (Proverbs 22:19), deepen our certainty of what defines truth, and provide sound answers when others depend on them (22:21). Proverbs represents but a slice of the entirety of God's revealed truth, and yet the challenge issued in this book applies to the whole Bible. "Prove yourselves doers of the word," James wrote, "and not merely hearers who delude themselves" (James 1:22).

Proverbs 23

Do not let your heart envy sinners,
But live in the fear of the LORD always.
Surely there is a future,
And your hope will not be cut off.   *—Proverbs 23:17–18*

Returning again to the book's theme, chapter 23 reminds us that living "in the fear of the Lord always" assumes a moment-by-moment contemplation and obedience. If only believers lived in the world, this command might seem easier. But instead we live in a culture with unbelievers who willingly surrender to the carnal temptations and materialistic trappings that believers are told to resist. What's hard is that they seem none the worse for it, which arouses envy in the hearts of God's people. To help us not "envy sinners," this proverb urges us to abandon our fixation with today's lack and to look to the promise of God's abundant future. Living in the fear of the Lord means fixing our hearts on what we know is coming and living with the hope that we, unlike unbelievers, "will not be cut off" (Proverbs 24:19–20; Hebrews 6:19; 10:23; 1 Peter 1:13).

Proverbs 24

My son, eat honey, for it is good,
Yes, the honey from the comb is sweet to your taste;
Know that wisdom is thus for your soul;
If you find it, then there will be a future,
And your hope will not be cut off.   *— Proverbs 24:13 – 14*

The command to eat honey was far from a dietary directive for the ancient Israelites. The act served as a memory trigger of spiritual truth. Five times the Proverbs use the term *honey* as a teaching device and only here in a positive way (Proverbs 5:3; 25:16, 27; 27:7). The sweetness of honey to the tongue illustrates the sweetness of wisdom to the soul. Finding wisdom means finding a life of hope with a certain and secure future. The New Testament links God's wisdom with God's Son and the hope He offers (1 Corinthians 1:30; 2 Timothy 3:15). The beauty of this proverb lies in its timeless application. Sweets usually concern parents and squelch diets. However, this proverb allows the moderate indulgence as a memory trigger to remind us of the sweetness that wisdom produces in our lives: "the hope of eternal life, which God, who cannot lie, promised long ages ago" (Titus 1:2).

Proverbs 25

These also are proverbs of Solomon which the men of Hezekiah,
king of Judah, transcribed.   *— Proverbs 25:1*

Proverbs contains only a portion of Solomon's sayings, for he "spoke 3,000 proverbs, and his songs were 1,005" (1 Kings 4:32).

Proverbs 25:1 isn't a proverb but rather an editorial note revealing that King Hezekiah commissioned his men to "transcribe" or to "move" some of Solomon's many proverbs from one scroll to another. Although this verse seems little more than a historical footnote, it actually offers a valuable insight into the doctrine of inerrancy. Hezekiah's scribes "moved" Solomon's words about 250 years after he wrote them, and yet the texts appeared in the original manuscripts of Proverbs without error. This reveals what logic also demands. Copies of Scripture are just as divinely authoritative as the original manuscripts as long as they reflect the originals. Even Jesus preached from copies of scrolls and yet called them "Scripture" (Luke 4:16–21). This offers us comfort and confidence as we base the certainty of our faith on the copies we hold today.

Proverbs 26

Do not answer a fool according to his folly,
Or you will also be like him.
Answer a fool as his folly deserves,
That he not be wise in his own eyes.   —*Proverbs 26:4–5*

These two proverbs stand back-to-back in order to reveal complementary, not contradictory, truths. In matters that don't matter, we should choose to ignore a foolish comment. To answer a fool "according to his folly" requires one to take on a fool's method and manner of speaking—to become a fool. On the other hand, sometimes a foolish statement "deserves" a response, lest our silence imply a tacit approval. Furthermore, without an answer that reveals the fool's mistake, this person will continue in error with the bloated assumption that "he is wise in his own eyes"—an attitude other proverbs in this chapter address (Proverbs 26:12, 16). Wisdom recognizes that sometimes it's better to say nothing, and on other occasions, it's foolish not to speak up. The apostle Paul had the latter in mind when he spoke "even as foolish" in order to silence the foolish thinking in Corinth (2 Corinthians 11:16–17).

Proverbs 27

Do not boast about tomorrow,
For you do not know what a day may bring forth. —*Proverbs 27:1*

To "boast" about tomorrow means literally to "praise" oneself (as rendered in Proverbs 27:2 and 27:21) as one who has confidence of what will occur. But this type of assertion is only an assumption, because no one knows "what a day may bring forth." The proverb isn't prohibiting wise planning—something the book urges repeatedly (Proverbs 11:14; 15:22; 20:18; 24:6). Rather, the verse cautions against self-confidence in planning, understanding that God alone knows the future and may indeed override our plans (16:1, 9; 19:21; 20:24). The apostle James developed this principle by urging his readers to make plans with humility: "You do not know what your life will be like tomorrow. You are just a vapor that appears for a little while and then vanishes away. Instead, you ought to say, 'If the Lord wills, we will live and also do this or that.' But as it is, you boast" (James 4:14–16).

Proverbs 28

He who trusts in his own heart is a fool,
But he who walks wisely will be delivered.   —*Proverbs 28:26*

Human depravity seeks (what it perceives as) its own good rather than the will of God. Ironically, God's will for His people *only* includes the best for them. "He who walks wisely" reads and obeys God's Word, which offers the only true course of wisdom. This biblical worldview flies in the face of the modern-day refrain "follow your heart," which—although it sounds noble and honoring to personal dignity—is terrible advice. Our hearts can deceive us . . . and often do (Isaiah 44:20; Jeremiah 17:9; 49:16). For this reason, Proverbs repeatedly warns us against the arrogance and ignorance of trusting in people—including ourselves—as opposed to trusting in God (Proverbs 3:5–6; 29:25). Verse 26 comes on the heels of "he who trusts in the LORD will be exalted" in verse 25, reminding us that we should maintain caution in our judgment and an unwavering confidence in God's.

Proverbs 29

Where there is no vision, the people are unrestrained,
But happy is he who keeps the law.   —*Proverbs 29:18*

A common misunderstanding of Proverbs 29:18 suggests that without "vision,"—that is, personal dreams and ambitions—"the people perish" (KJV). Modern-day translations offer a better rendering. The "vision" refers to divine revelation—Scripture—and the lack of that revelation leaves people "unrestrained." The latter term literally means to "let go, let loose" and is translated twice in Exodus 32:25 as "out of control." This context is instructive, for the Lord had just given the Ten Commandments to Moses, who descended from Sinai to find Israel "out of control." God's people need God's Word to bring order to their lives. But because the Lord created us as both spiritual and physical beings (Deuteronomy 8:3; Matthew 4:4), Scripture offers us more than simply a restraint against evil. God's Word provides the way to spiritual fulfillment; when we choose to "keep the law," we live "happy" (or "blessed") lives that bear the fruit of obedience.

Proverbs 30

Two things I asked of You,
Do not refuse me before I die:
Keep deception and lies far from me,
Give me neither poverty nor riches;
Feed me with the food that is my portion,
That I not be full and deny You and say, "Who is the LORD?"
Or that I not be in want and steal,
And profane the name of my God.   *— Proverbs 30:7–9*

Maintaining personal character forms the motivation for this two-pronged prayer by Agur. The first request reveals his sincere desire for integrity. Yet, Agur held an appropriate awareness of his own weakness, so his second request was for God to give him circumstances that would not tempt him to dishonor the Lord through either vanity or robbery. The two requests have one ultimate goal: a life of character that honors the Lord. Many of us today pray that God would give us prosperity and the wisdom to handle our finances well. But Agur's humble petition models the necessity of praying with our frailty in mind, asking that if riches would ever cause us to abandon God, He might be gracious enough to withhold them from us.

Proverbs 31

Charm is deceitful and beauty is vain,
But a woman who fears the LORD, she shall be praised.

— Proverbs 31:30

Written in Hebrew as an acrostic to aid memorization, the majority of Proverbs' final chapter presents the qualities of "an excellent wife" (Proverbs 31:10). The world idealizes a woman who has charm and beauty—short-term qualities that go only skin deep. But Scripture's definition of "excellent" begins and ends with a woman's character and her relationship with the Lord. Proverbs 31 reveals that a woman's godly character spills over into and blesses all aspects of her life—her marriage, her children, her home, her commercial interests, her teaching, and her town. The secret of her success? The theme of the entire book—she "fears the LORD." The New Testament echoes this emphasis by urging wives to focus on: "the hidden person of the heart, with the imperishable quality of a gentle and quiet spirit, which is precious in the sight of God" (1 Peter 3:4). As believers, we all—men and women alike—must make our internal character a higher priority than our external . . . and we must encourage others to do the same.

Ecclesiastes

Ecclesiastes 1

"Vanity of vanities," says the Preacher,
"Vanity of vanities! All is vanity." — Ecclesiastes 1:2

When the aged King Solomon reflected on his life and kingdom, he passionately proclaimed that it all was vanity—shallow, meaningless, and pointless. The king's stunning declaration opens Ecclesiastes and hovers over every sentence thereafter, casting a deathly pall over the intricate details of creation and the intimate circumstances of human lives he describes. Solomon had an acute sense of his own powerlessness to change the ways of the world. By highlighting its unchanging physical properties—the rising and setting sun, the blowing wind, and the flowing river (Ecclesiastes 1:5–7)—he underscored his lack of hope in himself. Truly, even the wisest man alive could not straighten out this crooked world (1:15). Solomon's words remind us of our own limited abilities to make lasting change in a fallen and broken world. The dire tone of Ecclesiastes 1 should awaken in us a yearning for God to work powerfully in this world and, ultimately, to send His Son to make all things new once again (Revelation 21:5).

Ecclesiastes 2

When there is a man who has labored with wisdom, knowledge and skill, then he gives his legacy to one who has not labored with them. This too is vanity and a great evil. — Ecclesiastes 2:21

Looking at some of life's most common pursuits through the lens of his own impending death brought clarity to Solomon. The old regent came to understand the pointlessness of pursuing pleasure (Ecclesiastes 2:1), wisdom (2:15), and work (2:21) for their own sakes. Objects obtained for pleasure fade and break down with age. The wise person will end up in the grave just like the fool. And the results from a person's hard work? They will be passed on to those who have not earned the results. So, accomplishment for its own sake, or even as a means to accumulate things we want, is pointless because it lacks good purpose. Work needs a worthy purpose behind it, a purpose that transcends ourselves. We must work as unto the Lord, laboring toward ends consistent with His purposes (Colossians 3:23). Only then, Solomon reminds us, will we find real and lasting enjoyment in this life (Ecclesiastes 2:25).

Ecclesiastes 3

He has made everything appropriate in its time. He has also set eternity in their heart, yet so that man will not find out the work which God has done from the beginning even to the end.

—Ecclesiastes 3:11

Birth and death, joy and mourning, peace and conflict—the human experience has its commonalities. But the variety of the details staggers the mind. Experiences vary from person to person and age to age. Amazingly, whoever, wherever, and whenever we might be, God sees to it that everything we experience comes at the appropriate time. However, while God's sovereignty is unquestioned and while we can appreciate God's presence in and through our circumstances, Solomon affirms that we will not have a full accounting of the Lord's work—neither in our own lives nor in all of human history (Ecclesiastes 3:11). In other words, the goal for us is to trust God by faith rather than follow by sight. Instead of seeking out an objective confirmation of God's working that He has not promised to reveal, let's prayerfully make decisions while trusting God to direct our paths (Psalm 37:23).

Ecclesiastes 4

Two are better than one because they have a good return for their labor. For if either of them falls, the one will lift up his companion. But woe to the one who falls when there is not another to lift him up.
—*Ecclesiastes 4:9–10*

We need each other. Solomon made it clear in Ecclesiastes that we live in a hard, often lonely world. As God indicated just after the creation of Adam (Genesis 2:18), human beings were not made to be alone. We were made for community. Solomon's acknowledgement of this reality in the context of shared labor makes a point many of us can immediately appreciate — not just intellectually but deep within our hearts. When we work, we get tired and disillusioned. Having another person share in our work can lift our spirits, giving us the energy to continue and finish the job. We need not limit to formal employment these kinds of shared partnerships. We need them in every facet of our lives. Everyone benefits when we allow family, friends, and colleagues to bear our burdens and vice versa. Paul taught that following this advice helps us fulfill Christ's ideal for His people (Galatians 6:2).

Ecclesiastes 5

Do not be hasty in word or impulsive in thought to bring up a matter in the presence of God. For God is in heaven and you are on the earth; therefore let your words be few. —*Ecclesiastes 5:2*

As Christians seeking to worship God with our whole selves, controlling our words has to be one of our most difficult tasks. We often speak too quickly for our own good, particularly when confronted with puzzling or overwhelming situations. At such moments, we fail to carefully consider what God wants for us. Instead, we tell Him what *we* desire. We speak rather than listen. King Solomon understood the danger of quick speech, knowing it can lead to poor listening skills and can negatively affect our actions. In this passage, Solomon wanted to show us that the approach to life that seeks out opportunities to listen rather than speak is the approach of a person who recognizes he or she lives under the authority of God. Every effort to control our tongues and listen is a recognition of our own smallness and God's greatness.

Ecclesiastes 6

A man might have a hundred children and live to be very old. But if he finds no satisfaction in life and doesn't even get a decent burial, it would have been better for him to be born dead.

—*Ecclesiastes 6:3 (NLT)*

Solomon believed that prosperity consists of having a long life and many offspring. Coming from a man who had access to anything he wanted, his prosperity list is surprisingly short. Possibly even more surprising, Solomon invoked the harsh and shocking image of a stillborn baby to describe the circumstances of the person who finds no joy in such prosperity. Having no life at all would be better than living a prosperous existence without enjoying it. We understand Solomon's negative example to include an implied positive exhortation: we should take joy in our own lives and in the lives of those who will continue on after we die. Further, Solomon's teaching reminds us of what's truly valuable in life — the opportunity to live many years and to be surrounded by our children. Rather than looking for joy in flashy new objects, expensive trips, or some other passing fancy, we should allow our joy to rest in God's greatest blessing: life.

Ecclesiastes 7

It is better to go to a house of mourning
Than to go to a house of feasting,
Because that is the end of every man,
And the living takes it to heart. — *Ecclesiastes 7:2*

When offered the choice to go to a feast or a funeral, most people would choose the celebration over the memorial. Solomon challenged that natural tendency — not because the king courted pain and death but because he understood that death makes people appreciate and consider life in ways that joyous celebrations do not. Solomon believed that the person constantly seeking the fulfillment of his or her own pleasures is a fool (Ecclesiastes 7:4). It is when life's difficulties force us to grapple with the hard realities of this fallen world that we gain wisdom. Solomon's perspective prompts us to face up to life's hardships, rather than run from them. We live in a culture with so many options for masking, or completely eliminating, pain that we can miss opportunities to confront it and grow through it.

Ecclesiastes 8

Although a sinner does evil a hundred times and may lengthen his
life, still I know that it will be well for those who fear God, who fear
Him openly. —*Ecclesiastes 8:12*

We have only to open our eyes and wickedness dances before us
in mocking victory. The pain that comes through watching the
triumph of suffering and death often strikes us as senseless and
without purpose. When wicked people find success, those of us
seeking to honor and glorify God find questions and uncertainty.
And while that tension will never go away on this side of God's
kingdom, Solomon reminded us that while we may struggle in
this life, things ultimately go well for those who fear God. When
we faithfully seek after God and follow His desires for our lives,
we can rest in the hope that we have a glorious future with Him
in heaven. We can alleviate discouragement by remembering
the positive vision of the future God has promised. Wickedness
is destined to surround human beings until the return of Jesus.
Rather than dwell on the evil we see around us, we can find
comfort in God's sustaining presence in our lives.

Ecclesiastes 9

It is the same for all. There is one fate for the righteous and for the
wicked; for the good, for the clean and for the unclean; for the man
who offers a sacrifice and for the one who does not sacrifice. As the
good man is, so is the sinner; as the swearer is, so is the one who is
afraid to swear. —*Ecclesiastes 9:2*

Everyone dies. Personal background? Doesn't matter. Gender,
race, religion? Beside the point. Wealthy or poor? Death will find
us in its time. Death travels to every corner of the globe looking

to devour all in its path. Humans go to extraordinary lengths to sidestep death's visitation. We change our diets, undergo medical procedures, and participate in religious rituals. And yet, the end of life draws ever nearer to all. We understand death as the ultimate equalizer—it brings us all low, humbles us before powers far beyond our own. Death reminds us that, in an ultimate sense, we have very little control over the direction of our lives. And when we approach them in the proper mind-set, the deaths of those we love can bring a sadness that prompts us to embrace the hope that believers have in Jesus. In this way, death affords us the opportunity to consider more carefully and prayerfully the choices we make in life.

Ecclesiastes 10

Woe to you, O land, whose king is a lad and whose princes feast in the morning. Blessed are you, O land, whose king is of nobility and whose princes eat at the appropriate time—for strength and not for drunkenness. —*Ecclesiastes 10:16–17*

Our actions impact our families and communities. But our deeds also affect the physical creation around us. Solomon's conclusion about the land is based on the people who live in it. Young and lazy leaders yield a woeful land, while noble and hard-working leaders produce a blessed land. While Solomon referred to leaders in particular, the truths contained in these verses apply to people of all stripes. No matter our social standing, our actions either take a toll upon or bring life to the physical creation around us. God's desire that we concern ourselves with the well-being of the created world goes all the way back to His command that Adam cultivate and keep the garden of Eden (Genesis 2:15). Are we being good stewards of creation? Solomon's blessing on the land prompts us to devote ourselves to the hard work of caring for the created world, and our concern for creation ultimately reflects our concern for others.

Ecclesiastes 11

Sow your seed in the morning and do not be idle in the evening, for you do not know whether morning or evening sowing will succeed, or whether both of them alike will be good. —*Ecclesiastes 11:6*

The days of doing only one job have long passed us by . . . if they ever existed in the first place. We work, in part, so that we can sustain ourselves and our families. This reality of God's world sets boundaries on how we spend our time. We have to work. Solomon's wisdom calls us to foster multiple opportunities rather than bank on a single uncertainty. Instead of simply attending to the tasks at our day jobs, we should consider how we might also support ourselves in other ways. When we commit to variety in our work, we increase our ability to provide for ourselves and others long-term—when one job ends, other venues are there to make up the lost wages. Solomon's good advice also serves to protect us from the pitfalls of laziness. When we fill our time with good actions, we're less likely to get pulled down by the temptations of sin.

Ecclesiastes 12

The conclusion, when all has been heard, is: fear God and keep His commandments, because this applies to every person.

—Ecclesiastes 12:13

In the book of Ecclesiastes, old King Solomon recorded his search for a meaningful life. He had tried to make pleasure, wisdom, or even work the ultimate goal of his life, but these pursuits—noble as they are—failed to bring meaning on their own. Instead, Solomon came to understand that we all need to turn our focus outward if any of us hope to find true meaning and significance in life. Therefore, as the aged king brought his writing to a conclusion, he summed up his advice in the simplest way possible: fear God and keep His commands. Finding something true and lasting and significant in this world of senseless suffering will come only as we direct our lives outward. Only when we serve God and the needs of others can we ever hope to have a sense of purpose that can flood the gaping hole of meaninglessness we experience in this fallen world (Matthew 22:36 – 40).

Song of
Solomon

Song of Solomon 1

"May he kiss me with the kisses of his mouth!
For your love is better than wine.
Your oils have a pleasing fragrance,
Your name is like purified oil." *— Song of Solomon 1:2–3*

The Song of Solomon begins with a desire for physical intimacy, expressed by a woman not yet married to Solomon. It wasn't simply that she wanted a kiss; she wanted *Solomon's* kiss. Why? Because his "name," or his reputation, was "like purified oil." This woman knew the rarity of meeting a man whose character is his most outstanding quality. And what was true in Solomon's day remains true today: character is what makes a person most attractive. The Bible repeatedly points to good character as the means by which success occurs in every realm. When the physical beauty of a romantic relationship fades, godly character carries it to the end. Therefore, character must be where we begin. Instead of trying to *find* the right person, Scripture urges us to *be* the right person and trust God to bring us the right match in His time. It's not a quest, but a discovery.

Song of Solomon 2

"Catch the foxes for us,
The little foxes that are ruining the vineyards,
While our vineyards are in blossom." *— Song of Solomon 2:15*

Foxes ruin a vineyard by burrowing and gnawing and damaging its fruit. In chapter 1, Solomon's fiancée referred to her body as a vineyard (Song of Solomon 1:6). So here, in chapter 2, a vineyard "in blossom" represents her maturity and readiness to marry. The foxes signify threats to their relationship that ought to be caught. During courtship, a couple should identify and eliminate potential problems—and count carefully the high cost of marriage. Budding troubles ignored before marriage are the seeds for major disappointments after marriage. Sex and security won't overshadow reality. Marriage and love bring a deeper capacity for joy, but they also carry a deeper potential for hardship and troubles (1 Corinthians 7:28). In the context of human relationships, marriage offers both the best and worst feelings a person can have. Matrimony has many hidden potential problems, and anyone who doesn't count the cost beforehand is in for a shock.

Song of Solomon 3

"I adjure you, O daughters of Jerusalem,
By the gazelles or by the hinds of the field,
That you will not arouse or awaken my love
Until she pleases."   —*Song of Solomon 3:5*

In the third chapter, Solomon's fiancée repeated a line she uttered earlier in their courtship—an expression that clearly represents a yearning for sexual intimacy (Song of Solomon 2:6–7). Along with her desire, however, Solomon's fiancée also had the wisdom of timing and restraint. She compelled Solomon not to "arouse or awaken my love until she pleases" (3:5). Further, she warned other young women to insist upon chastity and not intentionally arouse their men's desire until the right time—specifically, marriage. In each area of our lives, self-control helps us keep pure what God created to be pure and not step out of the bounds He has clearly given us in His Word. The helpful word *until* reminds every unmarried person that there is an appropriate time for arousal. All good gifts from God are worth the wait — including sex.

Song of Solomon 4

"A garden locked is my sister, my bride,
A rock garden locked, a spring sealed up. . . .
You are a garden spring,
A well of fresh water,
And streams flowing from Lebanon."   — *Song of Solomon 4:12, 15*

This chapter features Solomon's wedding day and the first time his fiancée is called a "bride." The scene illustrates by principle the ideal preparations for marital sex. To build intimacy and heighten his bride's anticipation, Solomon initiated romantic conversation and provided an environment free from distractions. He praised her for the fact that her "garden" and "spring" had remained locked and sealed — a metaphor for her purity. On their wedding day, however, she was a spring flowing with fresh water. Solomon's bride dressed in a way to provide visual and sensual incentive, and Solomon waited for her invitation before they consummated their marriage (Song of Solomon 4:16). The Bible veils this erotic scene behind metaphors that reveal that foreplay in the context of godly marriage is good and serves not just to prepare two bodies — but two persons — to become one.

Song of Solomon 5

"I have taken off my dress,
How can I put it on again?
I have washed my feet,
How can I dirty them again?
My beloved extended his hand through the opening,
And my feelings were aroused for him." — *Song of Solomon 5:3–4*

Mrs. Solomon's cool response to her husband's request to unlock the door (Song of Solomon 5:3) shows how a spouse's attitude can change after marriage. She refused to get up and help him. Rather than argue, Solomon tried to unlock the door himself, but he couldn't — so he left. She regretted her cool reaction and went searching for him (5:3–8). Here, Solomon's wife models a tremendous response. Though she was initially indifferent, she soon recognized the negative result of her coolness and pursued reconciliation. Just like courtship, every marriage has its "foxes." It's how we deal with them that makes the difference in marital harmony. A good marriage isn't one without conflict but one that's committed to reconciliation. The opposite of love isn't hate but indifference. How a couple handles their problems will determine if they grow closer or further apart. Humility is key.

Song of Solomon 6

"I am my beloved's and my beloved is mine." — *Song of Solomon 6:3*

The conflict of chapter 5 finds its reconciliation in chapter 6, which features the couple's affirmation of their commitment to each other and their gratitude for each other's good qualities.

Solomon responded to his wife's affirmation of their mutual commitment (Song of Solomon 6:3) by encouraging her with words almost identical to those he gave her on their wedding night. In spite of their conflict, his commitment hadn't changed (6:4–7). No member of a couple should ever have to fear rejection from the other, nor should the word *divorce* come up as a threat during a conflict. Only unconditional commitment gives the people in a marriage the security to solve problems—and the motivation to do so. Further, conflict brought on by indifference like that in chapter 5 can be tempered with gratefulness for a spouse's good qualities. Gratitude can change the mood and environment. A healthy marriage thrives on repeated affirmation of commitment and expressed admiration of character.

Song of Solomon 7

"Come, my beloved, let us go out into the country. . . .
There I will give you my love. . . .
Over our doors are all choice fruits,
Both new and old." —*Song of Solomon 7:11–13*

In chapter 7, Solomon's wife initiated a romantic excursion into the country—a time devoted to the exclusive purpose of renewing their love and deepening their relationship. Here we see the importance of cultivating romance even after marriage. Many couples wonder why they don't feel like they did when they were courting; it could be that they don't date like they did when they were courting. Solomon's wife even suggested they enjoy "choice fruits, both new and old"—a metaphor representing plans for their sexual relationship to remain new and creative. God created the sexual aspect of marriage to mature just as the relational aspect should. It's a package deal. God designed the whole relationship to get better and better. A husband and wife should make plans to continue to court one another regularly and creatively in every aspect of their relationship . . . and manage their time and money to make it happen.

Song of Solomon 8

"Love is as strong as death . . .
Its flashes are flashes of fire,
The very flame of the LORD.
Many waters cannot quench love,
Nor will rivers overflow it."   *—Song of Solomon 8:6–7*

Song of Solomon describes love as the strongest of feelings and the firmest of commitments. It is like the flame of the Lord that no amount of water can quench. Nothing can put out the fire of true love—even though a couple experiences conflict. Godly love is permanent. It never ever quits, because the power of love's devotion is backed by the power of God. The flame that can't be put out is the very fire of God. Many forces will come against love, but if God is in the commitment of both the husband and the wife, nothing can break them apart. This type of love is priceless (Song of Solomon 8:7); therefore, a husband and wife give it unconditionally—just as God gives His love. A love that is given freely and unconditionally is cherished and lasts. How essential that each marriage partner remains committed to this type of unquenchable love.

How to Begin a Relationship with God

The five, beautiful Wisdom Books in the Bible convey magnificent truths about God. When we face devastating losses as Job did or when we feel hounded by our enemies as David did or when we despair of life as Solomon did, we can identify with some of the struggles in these books. We see our own sin and frailty contrasted with God's holiness and power. God still speaks powerfully today through the Wisdom Books, and the entire Old Testament, to change lives. Through the good news found in His Word, the Lord breathes eternal life into humble hearts. From Genesis to Revelation, God reveals four essential truths we all must accept and apply to receive the life-transforming help He promises. Let's look at these four truths in detail.

Our Spiritual Condition: Totally Depraved

The first truth is rather personal. One look in the mirror of Scripture, and our human condition becomes painfully clear:

> "There is none righteous, not even one;
> There is none who understands,
> There is none who seeks for God;
> All have turned aside, together they have
>   become useless;
> There is none who does good,
> There is not even one." (Romans 3:10–12)

We are all sinners through and through—totally depraved. Now, that doesn't mean we've committed every atrocity known to humankind. We're not as *bad* as we can be, just as *bad off* as we can be. Sin colors all our thoughts, motives, words, and actions.

If you've been around a while, you likely already believe it. Look around. Everything around us bears the smudge marks of our sinful nature. Despite our best efforts to create a perfect world, crime statistics continue to soar, divorce rates keep climbing, and families keep crumbling.

Something has gone terribly wrong in our society and in ourselves—something deadly. Contrary to how the world would repackage it, "me-first" living doesn't equal rugged individuality and freedom; it equals death. As Paul said in his letter to the Romans, "The wages of sin is death" (Romans 6:23)—our spiritual and physical death that comes from God's righteous judgment of our sin, along with all of the emotional and practical effects of this separation that we experience on a daily basis. This brings us to the second marker: God's character.

God's Character: Infinitely Holy

How can God judge us for a sinful state we were born into? Our total depravity is only half the answer. The other half is God's infinite holiness.

The fact that we know things are not as they should be points us to a standard of goodness beyond ourselves. Our sense of injustice in life on this side of eternity implies a perfect standard of justice beyond our reality. That standard and source is God Himself. And God's standard of holiness contrasts starkly with our sinful condition.

Scripture says that "God is Light, and in Him there is no darkness at all" (1 John 1:5). God is absolutely holy—which creates a problem for us. If He is so pure, how can we who are so impure relate to Him?

Perhaps we could try being better people, try to tilt the balance in favor of our good deeds, or seek out methods for self-improvement. Throughout history, people have attempted to live up to God's standard by keeping the Ten Commandments or living by their own code of ethics. Unfortunately, no one can come close to satisfying the demands of God's law. Romans 3:20 says, "By the works of the Law no flesh will be justified in His sight; for through the Law comes the knowledge of sin."

Our Need: A Substitute

So here we are, sinners by nature and sinners by choice, trying to pull ourselves up by our own bootstraps to attain a relationship with our holy Creator. But every time we try, we fall flat on our faces. We can't live a good enough life to make up for our sin, because God's standard isn't "good enough"—it's *perfection*. And we can't make amends for the offense our sin has created without dying for it.

Who can get us out of this mess?

If someone could live perfectly, honoring God's law, and would bear sin's death penalty for us—in our place—then we would be saved from our predicament. But is there such a person? Thankfully, yes!

Meet your substitute—*Jesus Christ*. He is the One who took death's place for you!

> [God] made [Jesus Christ] who knew no sin to be sin on our behalf, so that we might become the righteousness of God in Him. (2 Corinthians 5:21)

177

God's Provision: A Savior

God rescued us by sending His Son, Jesus, to die on the cross for our sins (1 John 4:9–10). Jesus was fully human and fully divine (John 1:1, 18), a truth that ensures His understanding of our weaknesses, His power to forgive, and His ability to bridge the gap between God and us (Romans 5:6–11). In short, we are "justified as a gift by His grace through the redemption which is in Christ Jesus" (Romans 3:24). Two words in this verse bear further explanation: *justified* and *redemption*.

Justification is God's act of mercy, in which He declares righteous the believing sinners while we are still in our sinning state. Justification doesn't mean that God *makes* us righteous, so that we never sin again, rather that He *declares* us righteous—much like a judge pardons a guilty criminal. Because Jesus took our sin upon Himself and suffered our judgment on the cross, God forgives our debt and proclaims us PARDONED.

Redemption is Christ's act of paying the complete price to release us from sin's bondage. God sent His Son to bear His wrath for all of our sins—past, present, and future (Romans 3:24–26; 2 Corinthians 5:21). In humble obedience, Christ willingly endured the shame of the cross for our sake (Mark 10:45; Romans 5:6–8; Philippians 2:8). Christ's death satisfied God's righteous demands. He no longer holds our sins against us, because His own Son paid the penalty for them. We are freed from the slave market of sin, never to be enslaved again!

Placing Your Faith in Christ

These four truths describe how God has provided a way to Himself through Jesus Christ. Because the price has been paid in full by God, we must respond to His free gift of eternal life in total faith and confidence in Him to save us. We must step forward into the relationship with God that He has prepared for us—not by doing good works or by being a good person, but by coming to Him just as we are and accepting His justification and redemption by faith.

> For by grace you have been saved through faith; and that not of yourselves, it is the gift of God; not as a result of works, so that no one may boast. (Ephesians 2:8–9)

We accept God's gift of salvation simply by placing our faith in Christ alone for the forgiveness of our sins. Would you like to enter a relationship with your Creator by trusting in Christ as your Savior? If so, here's a simple prayer you can use to express your faith:

> *Dear God,*
>
> *I know that my sin has put a barrier between You and me. Thank You for sending Your Son, Jesus, to die in my place. I trust in Jesus alone to forgive my sins, and I accept His gift of eternal life. I ask Jesus to be my personal Savior and the Lord of my life. Thank You. In Jesus's name, amen.*

If you've prayed this prayer or one like it and you wish to find out more about knowing God and His plan for you in the Bible, contact us at Insight for Living Ministries. Our contact information is on the following pages.

We Are Here for You

If you desire to find out more about knowing God and His plan for you in the Bible, contact us. Insight for Living Ministries provides staff pastors who are available for free written correspondence or phone consultation. These seminary-trained and seasoned counselors have years of experience and are well-qualified guides for your spiritual journey.

Please feel welcome to contact your regional office by using the information below:

United States

Insight for Living Ministries
Biblical Counseling Department
Post Office Box 5000
Frisco, Texas 75034-0055
USA
972-473-5097, Monday through Friday,
8:00 a.m.–5:00 p.m. central time
www.insight.org/contactapastor

Canada

Insight for Living Canada
Biblical Counseling Department
PO Box 8 Stn A
Abbotsford BC V2T 6Z4
CANADA
1-800-663-7639
info@insightforliving.ca

Australia, New Zealand, and South Pacific

Insight for Living Australia
Pastoral Care
Post Office Box 443
Boronia, VIC 3155
AUSTRALIA
1300 467 444

United Kingdom and Europe

Insight for Living United Kingdom
Pastoral Care
PO Box 553
Dorking
RH4 9EU
UNITED KINGDOM
0800 787 9364
+44 (0)1306 640156
pastoralcare@insightforliving.org.uk

Resources for Probing Further

God doesn't want Christians to simply increase their knowledge about Him and His Word. Our heavenly Father wants His children to know Him more intimately and apply His Word more fully to our lives. A multitude of books exist that tell us what the Bible says, but finding resources to help us *apply* its principles to everyday life is a bit more challenging. So we have compiled a list of resources that won't just take up space in your bookcase—they will help you live out God's Word each day. Keep in mind as you read these books that we can't always endorse everything a writer or ministry says, so we encourage you to approach these and all other non-biblical resources with wisdom and discernment.

Insight for Living. *Insight's Bible Application Guide: Genesis– Deuteronomy—A Life Lesson from Every Chapter*. Plano, Tex.: IFL Publishing House, 2012.

Insight for Living. *Insight's Bible Application Guide: Joshua– Esther—A Life Lesson from Every Chapter*. Plano, Tex.: IFL Publishing House, 2013.

Insight for Living. *Insight's Old Testament Handbook: A Practical Look at Each Book*. Plano, Tex.: IFL Publishing House, 2009.

Morgan, G. Campbell. *Life Applications from Every Chapter in the Bible*. Grand Rapids: Fleming H. Revell, 1994.

Swindoll, Charles R. *David: A Man of Passion & Destiny*. Great Lives Series. Nashville: Thomas Nelson, 2008.

Swindoll, Charles R. *Job: A Man of Heroic Endurance*. Great Lives Series. Nashville: Thomas Nelson, 2004.

Swindoll, Charles R. *Living the Proverbs: Insight for the Daily Grind*. Brentwood, Tenn.: Worthy Publishing, 2012.

Swindoll, Charles R. *Living the Psalms: Encouragement for the Daily Grind*. Brentwood, Tenn.: Worthy Publishing, 2012.

Wiersbe, Warren W. *The Wiersbe Bible Commentary: Old Testament*. Colorado Springs: David C. Cook, 2007.

Wiersbe, Warren W. *With the Word: The Chapter-by-Chapter Handbook*. Nashville: Thomas Nelson, 1993.

Ordering Information

If you would like to order additional copies of *Insight's Bible Application Guide: Job—Song of Solomon—A Life Lesson from Every Chapter* or other Insight for Living Ministries resources, please contact the office that serves you.

United States

Insight for Living Ministries
Post Office Box 5000
Frisco, Texas 75034-0055
USA
1-800-772-8888
(Monday through Friday, 7:00 a.m.–7:00 p.m. central time)
www.insight.org
www.insightworld.org

Canada

Insight for Living Canada
PO Box 8 Stn A
Abbotsford BC V2T 6Z4
CANADA
1-800-663-7639
www.insightforliving.ca

Australia, New Zealand, and South Pacific

Insight for Living Australia
Post Office Box 443
Boronia, VIC 3155
AUSTRALIA
1300 467 444
www.insight.asn.au

United Kingdom and Europe

Insight for Living United Kingdom
PO Box 553
Dorking
RH4 9EU
UNITED KINGDOM
0800 787 9364
www.insightforliving.org.uk

Other International Locations

International constituents may contact the U.S. office through
our Web site (www.insightworld.org), mail queries, or by
calling +1-972-473-5136.